Painting and Weathering Railroad Models

Jeff Wilson

KALMBACH **K** BOOKS

About the author

Jeff Wilson, currently an associate editor at *Model Railroader,* has been on the magazine's editorial staff since 1991. His duties at the magazine include editing the monthly Paint Shop and Ask Paint Shop columns. That and his interest in detailing and painting locomotives and rolling stock led him to write this, his first, book. "Painting is an area of the hobby that many people are afraid of, but one that can make a tremendous difference in the realism of a model or layout. Although there have been a lot of good individual articles on painting and weathering, there hasn't been a good reference book that compiles that information in a single source."

Jeff got his start as a model railroader when he received a battery-powered toy train at the age of four. Like many other kids, he was eventually given Marx and Lionel O gauge train sets, making the jump to HO scale when he was 11. He's currently building an HO scale version of the Chicago, Burlington & Quincy's Mississippi River line in half of his basement.

In addition to modeling, Jeff enjoys photographing trains, both model and prototype. When away from trains, the native Minnesotan can generally be found throwing his body around on a softball field, volleyball court, ice hockey rink, golf course, or basketball court, or simply spending time with his wife, Sonja.

Art director and cover design: Kristi Ludwig
Designer: Mike Schafer

Printed in the United States of America

Publisher's Cataloging in Publication
(Prepared by Quality Books, Inc.)

Wilson, Jeff.
    Painting and weathering railroad models / Jeff Wilson.
    p. cm.
    Includes bibliographical references and index.
    ISBN 0-89024-215-1

    1. Railroads—Models. I. Title.

TF197.W55 1995   625.1'9
                         QBI95-20189

Contents

Introduction

Creating a good-looking, realistic finish on a locomotive or car is a fun and rewarding part of model railroading. Unfortunately, painting probably scares off more would-be modelers than any other area of the hobby. If you've never painted a model before, or if you've been displeased with previous efforts, the tips and techniques in this book will help you achieve the results you want.

Start by practicing the various techniques—brush-painting, airbrushing, and weathering—on a few old or inexpensive freight car shells. Once you feel comfortable, try a couple of "real" projects. Completing a couple of simple freight cars successfully will give you confidence to try more complex projects.

Don't be afraid to make mistakes. As with any motor activity, painting and airbrushing take practice and experience to perfect. Remember the first time you tried to hit a softball? Chances are that you didn't hit a home run in your first at bat. It's the same way with painting. Don't be discouraged if your first efforts aren't what you had hoped for. Keep practicing on small projects, and you'll acquire the skills you'll need to tackle that undecorated locomotive that's been tempting you!

Although most of the projects I describe are modeled in HO scale, the techniques and ideas are applicable to any scale. Along with numerous one-evening projects, like weathering freight cars or trackside structures, you'll also find some major projects, like painting a brass steam locomotive.

I can't claim originality for many of the techniques in this book. Some of these methods have been around for decades, but they may be new to you—and just what you've been looking for! I've given some old techniques new twists, and perhaps you'll do the same.

It may help you to look at this as a book of ideas, rather than a book of instructions that you must follow to the letter. The only way to really learn about painting is to pick up your brush and airbrush and experiment with them. Try various techniques that you see, read about, or think of—some will work, some won't, but you'll learn things either way.

Whether your goal is to create contest-quality models or to improve the realism of your layout, *Painting and Weathering Railroad Models* can help you toward that goal.

—*Jeff Wilson*

1 All about Paint

The basics of paint and color

Painting intimidates many modelers. Besides the actual process of applying paint, the great selection of types and brands of paint—not to mention color—can be overwhelming. This chapter offers some basic information on paint coatings and color, then explains the differences among various types of paint.

What is paint?

In the real world paint adds color to almost everything you see. More important, it protects and seals surfaces—it keeps metal from corroding and wood from rotting. In the world of model railroading you use paint to re-create miniature versions of locomotives, cars, structures, and details from prototype (real) railroads and scenes. You also use paint to re-create special effects, such as weathering.

There are many types of paint available, each designed for a specific use. As a modeler, you don't have to know the chemistry of paint manufacturing, but you should have a general understanding of paint properties.

Paint has four primary components: pigment, resin, solvent, and additives. The pigment provides color and opacity. The resin, or "binder," is the heart of the paint, forming the actual paint film. A solvent, or thinner, dilutes the paint and controls the flow characteristics, drying rate, and thickness of the paint film. Additives can include fillers and driers, as well as ingredients to provide scuff resistance, change flow characteristics, incorporate the pigment into the resin, improve adhesion, or alter other qualities.

Each ingredient influences the characteristics of the others. Since there are about 80 common solvents used with thousands of resins and additives, paint manufacturers can create a nearly infinite variety of coatings to match the requirements of specific applications.

Enamels, lacquers, and acrylics

Enamels can be water- or solvent-based. They dry by auto-oxidation—by contact with oxygen in the air. Although enamels typically dry to the touch fairly quickly, they take about a week to cure fully. Once cured, this type of paint resists chemicals well and provides a very tough finish—which makes it extremely difficult to remove. Because enamels dry hard, they're not very flexible.

The paint film of lacquers is deposited by the evaporation of the solvent. Lacquers generally dry hard and retain color and gloss well, but they aren't as resistant to chemicals as enamels.

Although acrylics are water-based, once the water evaporates and the paint hardens they cannot be dissolved again by water. Because they are generally nontoxic and clean up with water they are convenient to use.

Common watercolors (such as tempera paints) are not the same as acrylics. Once watercolors dry, they reflow if water is reapplied to them. Watercolors can be useful in modeling if you apply a clear finish directly over them.

Model paints

Several companies make paint designed specifically for railroad models. Paints such as Accu-Flex, Accu-paint, Floquil, Polly S, Pro Color, and Scalecoat are mixed to match the colors used by prototype railroads. Chapter 3 contains a list of these paints, including information on thinner, recommended airbrush thinning ratios, and spraying pressures.

Pactra and Testor are just two of the many companies who make paints that are useful in model railroading, although they are designed for car, plane, and ship models.

So what exactly is it that makes any of these model paints better than the paints you buy at a local hardware or paint store? Other than color, the main differences between general-use and model paints are the size of the particles of pigment and the thickness of the coating. Pigments in most general-use paints aren't as finely ground as pigments in model paints.

As a modeler, you evaluate paint on the basis of its properties. Here are a few of the properties essential to creating quality models:

• **Accurate color.** Since you may often model specific equipment of real railroads, accurate color is a necessity. All of the manufacturers listed in Chapter 3 make paints designed to match colors used by prototype railroads.

• **Thin paint coating.** To avoid obscuring the fine detail on your models, you'll need paint with finely ground pigment that will cover in thin coats.

• **Good adhesion.** You'll need paint that sticks to styrene and other plastics, brass, urethane, wood, and various types of metal. The paint shouldn't run, peel, crack, or blister.

Mike Danneman

Fig. 1-2. Santa Fe's yellow hasn't held up well on rebuilt Geep no. 2252, shown at Kansas City in September 1990.

• **Durability.** It's important that painted models stand up to normal handling, but unless your models are designed to be outside in the elements, this isn't as important as the other qualities.

Most popular model paints fill all these needs.

The importance of proper colors

Few factors influence the overall realism of a layout more than color. Gaudy, inaccurate colors on trains, buildings, roads, and scenery can make a layout look toylike. Characteristics such as shiny plastic bricks on buildings and glossy figures contribute to a lack of realism.

No aspect of painting causes more arguments among modelers than color. Color perception is highly subjective—everyone see colors differently. What you view as a satisfactory color match another person may consider unacceptable.

Let's say you're modeling a yellow and gray Union Pacific diesel locomotive, so you want the best match for Armour Yellow and Harbor Mist Gray. After purchasing samples of paints manufactured by different companies, you'll notice that although they're all fairly close in color, the shades vary slightly. Which one is the right color? The most likely answer is that they all are.

How can that be? For starters, prototype paint varies from batch to batch. A barrel of Armour Yellow that DuPont mixed for the UP in 1990 may

be slightly different from a barrel mixed in 1992. Model paint can also vary slightly among batches.

Paint shades also vary among manufacturers. For example, a mid-1970s painting diagram for Amtrak diesels lists paint specification numbers for three paint manufacturers: DuPont, PPG (Pittsburgh Plate Glass), and Sherwin-Williams. Paint from these companies inevitably will vary slightly in shade, and each will weather differently because each company uses different resins and additives.

Over the years, paint from a single manufacturer can vary because of changes made to paint formulas—for example, because of the elimination of lead from paint.

Weathering

Depending on brand, color, and durability, paints weather differently. Many yellows, such as Chicago & North Western's Safety Yellow, Santa Fe's Warbonnet Yellow, and UP Armour Yellow, fade to near-white, as fig. 1-2 shows. Some reds turn orange; others fade to pink. These color changes can be quick or gradual. Quite often, the paint appears to be clean and unblemished, even though the color has faded from its original shade.

Type and amount of light

In addition to the various ingredients used to make paint, light is also a major influence in our perception of color. Here are some things to keep in mind when you're looking at a paint

sample, color print, transparency, or book photo:

• **Amount of light.** Color varies greatly depending on whether you see it in bright or dim light. Dark blues and greens often appear black in dim light. If you're painting a model of a dark blue Chesapeake & Ohio diesel that you saw outdoors in bright sunlight, you'll be disappointed if you use an exact paint match on a model that you'll see in a dimly lit basement.

• **Type of light.** Different types of light skew color. For example, bright sunlight at midday contains a large amount of blue, while sunlight near sunrise or sunset has more red and orange. Indoor lighting varies a great deal. Standard incandescent lighting generally has a lot of red and orange. Fluorescent lighting contains a lot of green, but the color varies greatly between "warm" and "cool" fluorescent lights.

To complicate things even more, some paints match others perfectly under one type of light, but not another.

Variables in film and printing

Beware of matching paint to a color print or a photo in a book. The lighting variables listed above are reason enough to be cautious. Additionally, color prints aren't reliable for color matching because they are second-generation images. That is, a print goes through two processing steps: first the film is developed, then a print is made from the negative. Each step can alter the color.

Another problem is that prints are extremely vulnerable to fading by ultraviolet light and chemical reactions. They begin fading right after they're made; colors change and wash out significantly over time.

Color photos in books can be unreliable because they are at least third-generation images. When publishers reproduce color images, the images are "separated" into tiny blue, yellow, black, and red dots. The quality of the separation can affect the color. The process of printing can change the color even further, depending upon the quality of ink and how heavily each color is applied.

Fig. 1-3. DuPont paint samples, Canadian National Ry. color standard samples, and a Bowles color drift card for Pennsylvania RR Dark Green "Brunswick Green" Locomotive Enamel appear from left to right.

Original color slides, depending upon the type of processing, can render color fairly accurately provided they are viewed in the proper light and are stored properly. Kodak's Kodachrome slide film renders colors well and has proven to be stable over time. I've seen 45-year-old Kodachrome slides that still have rich, true colors. Older Ektachrome and other films that use the E-6 developing process have not been as durable. Many images taken on Ektachrome professional film in the 1950s and '60s have begun to fade.

Another problem with slides (and prints) is the exposure. If slides are underexposed, colors can shift, and if a slide is overexposed, colors appear faded.

If you've been in the hobby for a while, you'll hear many modelers talking about the relative accuracy of certain model paints. "That's not even close," some will say. "I remember seeing those engines 20 years ago, and the blue was much brighter," others will proclaim. The truth is that memory is often faulty, and with a few exceptions, model paints are generally quite close to the colors they're meant to represent.

Checking color accuracy

Prototype railroads use color drift cards and paint chips, shown in fig. 1-3, to check the accuracy of paint colors.

That's fine for real railroads, but is that degree of accuracy really essential for modelers? Don't get hung up on finding the impossible "perfect match" and don't worry too much if your model colors vary a bit. Look at many sources—books, slides, and real locomotives—then choose a model color that looks good under the type of lighting your layout uses, and stick with it.

Primers

Primers can serve several purposes. It's important to know the properties of each and know when—or more important, when not—to use it. Most primers are designed to cover well and provide a uniform color for succeeding coats of paint. Most are flat, to give the following coat some "tooth" to grab onto. After that there are important differences.

Many modelers automatically use primers because they think a primer will stick to brass or plastic better than other paints. Unfortunately, this isn't always true, and all too often a primer becomes an unnecessary detail-hiding extra coat of paint. Some primers contain fillers, are sandable, and are designed for sealing and filling small imperfections on porous surfaces, such as wood or rough white-metal castings. Floquil's gray Primer is a good example. Because such primers contain fillers, they go on thicker than ordinary paint and can hide detail. Because of this, primers with fillers should not be used on brass or plastic models.

Other primers, such as Floquil's Zinc Oxide Primer, contain ingredients to inhibit rusting. This is fine for ferrous materials, but unnecessary for brass. Modelers often use this paint as a primer on brass, and although it provides a uniform base color it doesn't stick to brass any better than any other paint in the Floquil line.

Fig. 1-4. If you are spraying a brighter color on a dark surface, an initial coat of gray paint will give you a more accurate color.

Some primers, such as Accu-Flex Primer Gray, don't include fillers—they're just gray paint designed with high opacity so that they cover well.

So when should you use a primer on a brass or plastic model? For the most part, you really only need a primer to provide a uniform base color. If you're using a final paint color with good covering qualities, such as black, dark blue or green, maroon, or gray, you probably don't need a primer. Also, if you're painting a surface (such as a locomotive shell) that's already a uniform light color, a primer isn't necessary.

If you're spraying a brighter color, such as yellow, orange, or bright red, on a dark surface (such as a black plastic shell) or a surface with multiple colors (a gray shell with brass and black plastic details added, for instance), an initial coat of gray paint will give you a more accurate final color, as shown in fig. 1-4.

The covering quality of paints varies among brands. You can test these qualities on a piece of cardstock or scrap material. In general, it's better to apply one coat of primer and one or two coats of final color, rather than three or four solid coats of a final color.

Mixing and matching colors

Even though model paints are available in hundreds of colors, sometimes it's still necessary to do some adjusting to get the color you're looking for.

The color wheel in fig. 1-5 on the next page shows the relationship of

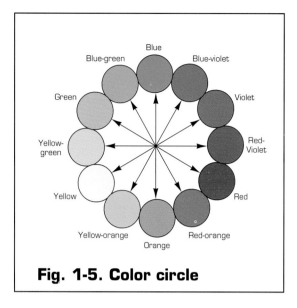

Fig. 1-5. Color circle

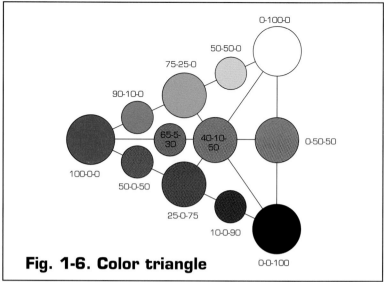

Fig. 1-6. Color triangle

colors to each other and can serve as a guide for mixing colors. The color triangle in fig. 1-6 is a guide to adjusting the shade and tone of any single color. It shows how adding white and black will alter the original color.

Both of these guides illustrate relationships among pure colors. The problem with mixing model paints is that they're not pure: most are already blends of other colors.

Many modelers try to match paint on commercial models, either to touch up a scratch or to paint another model to match the first one. Unfortunately, there's no magic formula for this. Find the closest model paint you can, then consult the color wheel and triangle and tweak the color by adding a bit of another color.

Eyedroppers are handy for measuring small amounts of paint, and toothpicks work well for mixing, as shown in figs. 1-7 and 1-8. If you're testing several mixes, be sure to label each one as shown in fig. 1-9. Keep a record of the paint mixes you use on your models—you'll be glad you did when you want to paint another model the same color.

Compatibility of paints and thinners

Never mix two different brands of paint, and never mix different types of paint (acrylics and lacquers, for example), even if they're made by the same company. The resins and solvents won't be compatible, and the result can be paint that doesn't mix properly, doesn't dry hard when cured, and sometimes doesn't cure at all.

For the same reasons, it's wise to use only thinners that are designed for specific paints. Thinners for non-water-based paints are made by mixing various solvents, such as acetone, methyl ethyl ketone, mineral spirits, toluene, xylene, and various alcohols. To achieve specific paint properties, manufacturers careful-

ly match the evaporation rates and other characteristics of these solvents to the properties of the resin.

As an example, common lacquer thinner has a different combination of solvents than Floquil's Dio-Sol or Airbrush Thinner. Consequently, using lacquer thinner with Floquil paints can affect the drying and curing time, adhesion, hardness of the paint film, and other characteristics. You might get a good finish—but you might not.

Manufacturers' thinners don't cost much more than common thinners (especially if you buy the larger economy containers), and the consistent results will be worth the expense. However, common lacquer thinner is handy and inexpensive for cleaning brushes and airbrush equipment after using solvent-based paints.

Now that you've read about the characteristics of paint, let's move to Chapter 2 and look at some of the equipment you'll need to apply it.

Fig. 1-7. To test mixes of paint, use an eyedropper to count drops of paint onto a piece of plain styrene or glossy cardboard.

Fig. 1-8. Use a toothpick to mix the paint thoroughly.

Fig. 1-9. Be sure to label each test piece with the paint formula for future reference.

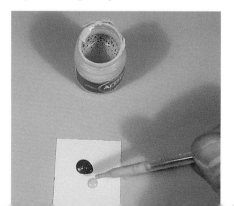

2 Equipment and Safety

Using airbrushes, compressors, and spray booths; working safely with solvents

Whether you're airbrushing or brush-painting, always keep your safety in mind when you paint. Many paints contain petroleum distillates and other organic solvents that can cause serious nervous-system and respiratory damage. People often ask if these paints are indeed safe to use. The answer is yes—but only if you take the proper precautions.

Safety with solvents

Try to avoid getting paint on your skin. Paint is not only irritating and difficult to get off, but it can cause damage to your skin. If you do get paint on your hands, don't use paint thinner (including mineral spirits, lacquer thinner, or Dio-Sol) to remove it. Paint thinners have very low surface tension, which means that your body readily absorbs them through the skin. Instead, use hand soap such as Lava and a brush to scrub the paint off, or use an industrial hand cleaner such as Goop, which is sold at many hardware and automotive stores.

The best way to keep paint off your hands is to wear rubber gloves. Paint thinners dissolve most ordinary latex rubber gloves, but Nitrile rubber gloves resist thinner and other chemicals. You can find these at hardware and paint stores under various brand names.

You should also avoid inhaling paint solvent vapor. The odor is not only irritating to you and your family, it can also do serious damage to your body. Any time you open a bottle of solvent-based paint or thinner, be sure to provide adequate ventilation and wear a face mask with two-stage filtration, also known as a respirator. Figure 2-1 shows one model. Ordinary dust masks provide no protection against solvent vapor. You should also avoid breathing alcohol-based thinners, even though they're not as dangerous as organic solvents.

Fig. 2-1. A chemical-cartridge mask, such as the one at left from American Optical, is a necessity when working with organic solvents. The dust mask at right will keep you from breathing paint particulates but doesn't offer any protection against solvent vapors.

Besides avoiding the health risks associated with solvents, take precautions against fire. Paint thinners and their vapors are extremely flammable. Do not use these paints in a room with an open flame, such as a pilot light for a water heater, furnace, stove, or gas dryer. Solvent vapors are generally heavier than air, which means they collect near floor level—where most pilot lights are located. Never smoke with open bottles of solvent-based paint or thinner around. Fig. 2-2 lists the solvents that are used in the various model paint thinners.

Many modelers are aware of the precautions that should be taken when airbrushing, but it is equally important to be careful when brushing lacquer-based paints. If you can smell the solvent, that means it is being absorbed into your system. Remember that just because a paint is plastic-compatible doesn't mean it's safe for humans. Many model paints that are safe to brush on plastics still contain potentially harmful solvents.

Airbrushing safety

First off, never—that means *never*—airbrush an organic-solvent-based paint indoors unless you use a spray booth that is vented outdoors. This warning applies to spray cans as well. Simply opening a window, even with a fan in it, is not enough to safely get rid of the solvent vapors.

When airbrushing with water-based paints there generally aren't any harmful vapors, but you should avoid breathing the paint particulates, which can irritate your throat and lungs. Wear a dust mask or respirator. It's also a good idea to use a spray booth to keep any overspray away from you and your models.

Some modelers use an ordinary cardboard box in an attempt to catch overspray. This arrangement usually doesn't work well. Overspray can bounce back from the rear and top and coat your model—and you—with tacky and dusty overspray, preventing you from getting a good finish on a model.

Fig. 2-2. Safety with organic solvents

Organic (carbon-based) solvents found in paints and thinners can do serious harm if you inhale them or absorb them through the skin. Here's a partial list of the solvents found in some model paints and thinners:

Product	Solvents included
Accu-paint thinner	acetone, methyl ethyl ketone
Floquil Dio-Sol, airbrush thinner	naphtha, toluene, xylene
Scalecoat thinner, Scalecoat II thinner	naphtha, xylene
clear coats and other lacquers	acetone, toluene, xylene
common lacquer thinner	methyl ethyl ketone, methyl isobutyl ketone, toluene

Short-term effects of high-level exposure to these solvents include breathing difficulty, dizziness, fatigue, nausea, and headaches. Severe cases can result in loss of consciousness and respiratory failure. Obviously, if you experience any of the initial symptoms, get into fresh air immediately and take steps to see that the exposure isn't repeated. Seek medical attention promptly if any symptoms persist.

Long-term effects of contact with dangerous levels of the solvents can include deterioration of bone marrow, blood disorders, and nervous system damage.

These products can be used safely. By providing adequate ventilation (a spray booth) and wearing an approved respirator, such as the one in fig. 2-1, you can keep exposure to these chemicals well within safe levels. Look for a chemical-cartridge respirator that fits your face properly and doesn't allow any air in except through the filters. The masks are available in several styles and sizes. Follow the manufacturers' directions regarding proper fitting and maintenance.

Safety labels on paints and thinners usually list the type of chemical cartridge needed to protect you from that product's ingredients. For most of the solvents listed above, a TC-23C cartridge (or equivalent) approved by NIOSH and MSHA is recommended. This number can be found on the cartridge itself as well as on the packaging for the mask and cartridge.

Eye protection is also a must when working with solvents. A stray splash or spray of solvent can easily injure your eyes, so a pair of safety goggles should be standard equipment.

This information isn't designed to scare you away from solvent-based paints. However, it's important to understand the need for safety and the methods you should take to protect yourself and your family.

Solvent disposal
Never dispose of your old thinner or paint by pouring it down a drain. Also refrain from sneaking out to the back yard and dumping it behind the garage.

Use an old solvent can (never a glass container) to collect old paint and solvents. Many local municipalities have special collection dates for hazardous materials once or twice a year. Others require these materials to be dropped off at a central location.

Modelers in warm climates have the option of doing their painting outdoors, but not everyone is so lucky. If you plan to do a lot of airbrushing, a spray booth is almost a necessity.

Setting up a spray booth

Fig. 2-3 shows the components of a typical spray booth. Good-quality booths, such as the North Coast Prototype Models booth in fig. 2-4, are available commercially. It's also possible to build your own.

A booth should have a squirrel-cage fan with its motor outside the air-flow path. Common bathroom and kitchen exhaust fans usually have a motor in the air path, making them unsuitable.

The fan must move enough air through the booth to remove all of the solvent vapor and paint particulates. The Occupational Safety and Health Administration (OSHA) recommends an air flow of 100 to 200 cubic feet per minute (cfm) as a safe rate for spraying organic solvents. Fig. 2-5 explains how to calculate the air flow for any given fan and booth size.

The booth must be vented to the outside via its own duct. Don't use a Y-joint to combine it with a dryer vent. These joints inevitably leak one way or another, and you don't want dryer lint in your spray booth or solvent vapors in your dryer! When you install a spray booth it's usually easiest to replace a window pane with a piece of wood, then add a vent and ductwork.

Keep the duct path as straight and short as possible. Many solvents will attack plastic and vinyl ductwork, so use only metal parts. Corrugated (flexible) ductwork will restrict airflow and reduce your fan's efficiency, so be sure to use smooth ductwork. You won't want to use a spray booth in a tightly sealed room, so you'll need to provide a source of incoming air by opening a window or door.

Also make sure that you keep light fixtures away from the paint spray. A booth with a clear acrylic panel on top with a light mounted above it is ideal.

Once you begin to use your booth, replace your filter frequently. Paint particulates collect in the filter and gradually reduce the fan's effectiveness.

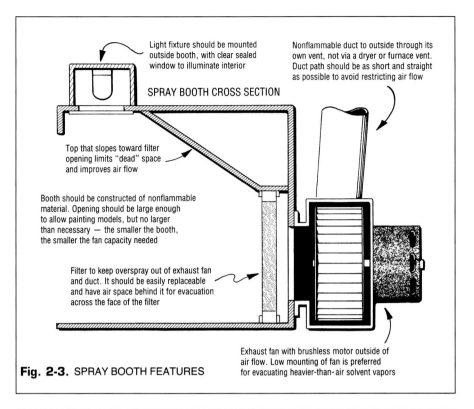

Light fixture should be mounted outside booth, with clear sealed window to illuminate interior

Nonflammable duct to outside through its own vent, not via a dryer or furnace vent. Duct path should be as short and straight as possible to avoid restricting air flow

SPRAY BOOTH CROSS SECTION

Top that slopes toward filter opening limits "dead" space and improves air flow

Booth should be constructed of nonflammable material. Opening should be large enough to allow painting models, but no larger than necessary — the smaller the booth, the smaller the fan capacity needed

Filter to keep overspray out of exhaust fan and duct. It should be easily replaceable and have air space behind it for evacuation across the face of the filter

Exhaust fan with brushless motor outside of air flow. Low mounting of fan is preferred for evacuating heavier-than-air solvent vapors

Fig. 2-3. SPRAY BOOTH FEATURES

Fig. 2-5 spray booth fan capacity

If you're building a spray booth, it's important to know how to calculate the size of the fan you need to maintain an air flow of 100 to 200 cubic feet per minute (cfm). Most exhaust fans are rated in cubic feet per minute (cfm). Two examples are Dayton's 4C445A, rated at 525 cfm, and 2C946 (815 cfm). Other companies sell comparable models.

Here are the two formulas you need to know:

• Booth opening in square inches ÷ 144 = opening in square feet

and

• Fan rating in cfm ÷ booth opening in square feet = air flow

As an example, let's say you have a booth with a 15" x 24" front opening. Multiplying 15 by 24 gives a booth opening of 360 square inches. Dividing that by 144 tells you that the opening is 2.5 square feet.

If you plan to use a 525 cfm fan, divide 525 by 2.5 and get an air flow of 210 cfm, which should be sufficient. It's always a good idea for the air flow to be on the high side of the safe range, because forcing air through the ductwork and filter can reduce the fan's capacity by 20 cfm or more.

Fig. 2-4. This commercial North Coast Prototype Models booth will have you airbrushing in a short time.

Air supplies

If you do a lot of airbrushing you'll need a consistent source of air. The small cans of propellant shown in fig. 2-6 are inadequate for most uses, as they last for only 10 to 15 minutes.

Regulating the pressure of propellant cans can be a challenge, and they're expensive. You're usually better

off taking the money you'd spend on a year's supply of propellant cans and applying it toward a compressor or other source of air.

Compressors: Most companies that sell airbrushes also sell compressors. Badger, Paasche, and W. R. Brown all sell small compressors that range from $100 to $200 in price. Figure 2-7 shows one example. Be sure to buy one

that provides at least 35 pounds of pressure (needed for some water-based paints). Some small piston compressors can provide only 20 psi. If you're able to spend a bit more money, silent compressors are great to have. Badger and Binks sell several models that are about as quiet as a refrigerator.

A combination compressor/tank is also nice, because a reservoir tank eliminates the "pulsing" that can occur if you connect your airbrush directly to a compressor. The tank also eliminates the need for the compressor to run continuously.

In addition, you'll need two more accessories: a regulator and a moisture trap, as shown in fig. 2-8. The regulator controls the air flow. Compressors condense water vapor from the air, and a moisture trap removes the water before it comes out of your airbrush and splatters your model. Some compressors have these features built into them.

Air and CO₂ tanks: Some modelers use low-pressure tanks as an air source. They eliminate the noise of a compressor, but you still need to recharge them periodically. It can be frustrating to run out of air on Friday night if you can't get your tank refilled until Monday.

An ordinary 5-gallon air tank charged to 100 pounds will give you enough air to spray continually for about five to ten minutes, depending upon the airbrush pressure. Since airbrushing involves intermittent use, this supply should be enough to paint two or three average models. Larger tanks are available but become quite cumbersome if you have to haul them up and down a stairway when they need to be recharged.

Air tanks are available at hardware stores (you'll need to add a regulator/moisture trap) and filled up at service stations. Although they can be a hassle, a tank can be a good low-cost alternative to compressors and propellant cans if you don't use your airbrush that often.

High-pressure air tanks are another air source. These tanks, like the one in fig. 2-9, can often be purchased used through fire equipment companies, scuba diving shops, welding-supply dealers, and other compressed-gas dealers. The tank in the photo can hold a charge of 1,800 pounds of air, which will keep most modelers painting for several weeks.

These tanks are more expensive than low-pressure tanks because they are stronger and must be tested periodically. You'll also need to add some special plumbing to regulate the air. Most scuba-diving shops and some welding

shops can recharge these tanks. A system like this can end up costing as much as a small compressor, but the result is a quiet source of air.

Another alternative is a high-pressure carbon dioxide (CO₂) tank. These look like the high-pressure air tanks and have many of the same advantages and disadvantages. Be aware that CO₂ can sometimes dry paint

(especially acrylics) too quickly. Modelers using CO₂ adapt to this characteristic by thinning paint a bit more or adding retarder.

These tanks are generally safe, but many people feel uncomfortable having high-pressure tanks in their house. If you choose either of these options, be sure to purchase your tank from a reputable dealer and have the

Fig. 2-6 (above left). It's difficult to regulate the pressure from expensive cans of propellant like this. Fig. 2-7 (above right). This compressor from W. R. Brown includes a built-in tank.

Fig. 2-8. These accessories are vital for controlling pressure and keeping water droplets off your model.

Fig. 2-9. Tanks like these can hold a charge of 1,800 psi, but can cost as much as a good compressor.

tank inspected as often as required (at least annually).

Other air sources: Resourceful modelers have used many other sources, from spare car tires to garden-type pump sprayers. Nearly all of these can be difficult to use, so it's usually easiest in the long run to invest in a more dependable source of air.

Airbrushes

The airbrush is the heart of any painting system. Quality models are available from Badger, Binks, Paasche, Thayer & Chandler, W. R. Brown, and others. Selecting an airbrush is largely a matter of personal taste. Find one that fits your hand comfortably and feels well-balanced when you hold it. Your hand, finger size, and strength of both influence what you select. Make sure that the paint jar (or color cup) and air hose don't interfere with a comfortable grip on the airbrush.

Most airbrushes work by forcing air over a tube that extends into a paint jar or cup, which siphons paint up into the airbrush, as shown in fig. 2-10. (Other models work by gravity feed.) The paint and air are combined and the paint is atomized into fine particles by forcing it past the tip of a needle. The air pushes the paint out of the airbrush and onto the painted surface.

Types of airbrushes

Figure 2-11 shows a typical external-mix airbrush. These airbrushes mix the paint and air outside of the airbrush body. The color control tip includes the needle, which passes up through a cone. Turning the cone, which is threaded onto the needle, adjusts the amount of paint drawn through it.

External-mix airbrushes are fairly easy to use. They're also easy to clean because their parts are readily accessible. These are all "single-action" airbrushes, meaning that the trigger regulates only the air flow.

Internal-mix brushes, shown in fig. 2-12, mix paint and air inside the body. They come in both single- and

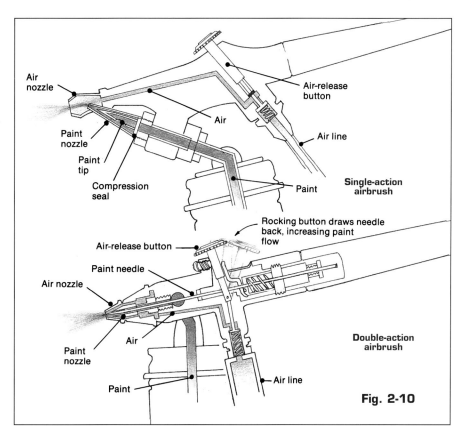

Fig. 2-10

Fig. 2-11. This Paasche H is typical of external-mix airbrushes.

Fig. 2-12. This Badger no. 150 is a double-action brush, so the trigger controls both air and paint flow.

Fig. 2-13. If the needle is bent or if the cone is flared outward, bent, or cracked, the result will be spattered, poorly atomized paint.

double-action versions. With a double-action airbrush, the trigger performs two functions: pushing down regulates the air flow, and pulling back draws the paint.

Internal-mix models are more prone to clogging and not as easy to clean, since you must disassemble the airbrush to reach all of the parts. Try to avoid bending the long, fine needle in these brushes or damaging the tip. If the needle or tip is bent or damaged in any way, paint will no longer flow properly, resulting in a poor paint finish.

Figure 2-13 shows an external-mix control tip that was damaged when it hit the floor. It's sometimes possible to straighten a bent tip by rolling it against a hard surface, and a cone that's bent on one side can sometimes be reshaped by screwing the needle assembly firmly into it. However, the results are often not perfect, so it's best to buy a replacement part. It's also wise to have a spare handy.

You can achieve a good-quality paint finish with either type of airbrush. Internal-mix airbrushes produce finely atomized paint particles, which can provide a smoother paint surface. Double-action brushes provide excellent control, which is very handy when you're doing detail work or weathering. However, they are more difficult to use—and it may take longer to get used to the feel of controlling both air and paint with the trigger.

External-mix brushes are fine for most general work, but I use a double-action internal-mix airbrush for weathering, especially when spraying thinned mixtures. You'll learn more about that in the next chapter.

Cleaning your airbrush

A good airbrush can last a lifetime, but like any precision tool, careless handling can ruin it. Thoroughly cleaning the airbrush after each painting session is an excellent habit to acquire.

If you spray a few different colors during a single painting session you might be able to get away with simply spraying thinner through the airbrush between colors. However, to make sure you don't contaminate any colors, it's best to clean it completely. Your airbrush owner's manual will include instructions, but here are the basics:

If you're spraying from a bottle, remove the paint jar and screw a jar of thinner (water or lacquer thinner, depending on the type of paint) in its place. Hold a paper towel against the air hole in the cap, then swish the thinner around vigorously.

If you're using a color cup, dump any unused paint in a storage container, then add some thinner to the cup with an eyedropper.

Spray the thinner through the airbrush while turning the color control tip (or needle adjustment) back and forth,

varying the spray from fine to broad. Continue spraying until the thinner flowing through the airbrush is clear.

Remove the bottle of thinner or color cup and use a paper towel to clean out the inside of the bottle cap. Run a pipe cleaner saturated with thinner through the siphon tube on the cap assembly or down the tube into the color cup.

On an external-mix brush, remove the color control tip and use a pipe cleaner dipped in thinner to clean the needle inside and the cone. Don't force the pipe cleaner through the hole in the cone tip or the hole in the middle of the needle. When you're finished, wipe off the parts with a paper towel.

With an internal-mix brush, use a cotton swab dipped in thinner to clean the siphon opening at the bottom of the brush. Unscrew the spray regulator and clean the opening, making sure that the holes on the outer tube are open and that there's no paint buildup near the needle opening. Use a paper towel to gently clean off the tip of the needle.

When you use cotton swabs or pipe cleaners in cleaning your airbrush, they can leave bits of fuzz behind—which can wind up mixed in your next batch of paint. Examine the parts carefully when you're finished cleaning to make sure they're clear of fuzz.

Cleaning up solvent-based paints requires a different approach than

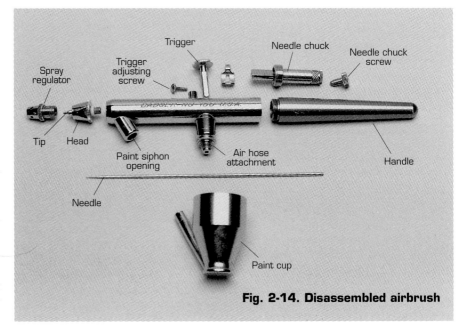

Fig. 2-14. Disassembled airbrush

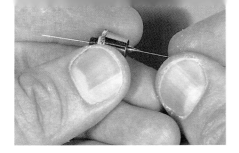

Fig. 2-15. Brass wire will sometimes free paint stuck in the tip of an internal-mix brush.

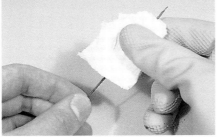

Fig. 2-16. Pull the needle repeatedly through a paper towel wet with lacquer thinner. Protect your hand with a Nitrile rubber glove.

acrylics. With lacquers, a few minutes of time aren't critical, since thinner will remove dried paint with no problems. However, acrylics set quickly, and once cured they become impervious to their thinner (water). It's therefore very important to get acrylic paint off airbrush parts before the paint has time to set.

Be sure to wear Nitrile rubber gloves when cleaning up with lacquer thinner. If you're using water-based paint, a pair of plain latex rubber gloves will help you avoid getting paint on yourself.

You're finished cleaning when there are no signs of the last color you sprayed. If you care for your equipment this well, your airbrush will give you years of good service.

Troubleshooting

One advantage of an external-mix brush is its simplicity—problems are usually fairly obvious. If a problem occurs, it's generally around the needle tip and cone. As I mentioned earlier, even a slightly bent needle or dented cone can cause paint spattering.

Internal-mix airbrushes are more complex. Figure 2-14 shows one partially disassembled. Once again, the needle and its nozzle are the keys to the system. If the airbrush seems to be plugged, or if the needle doesn't spring back into position (on a double-action brush), disassemble the tip and check the head and tip.

Figure 2-15 shows how to free dried specks of paint with a wire. Do this carefully so the tip is not damaged. If the clog is serious, you'll have to ream the tip. Badger sells a reamer designed for the purpose.

Paint can also build up inside the brush on the needle. To clean this buildup, unscrew the needle from the rear of the brush and slowly pull it out of the airbrush. Keep the body upright, because the needle holds the trigger and springs in alignment—tip the airbrush and these parts will fall out.

Now wet a paper towel in lacquer thinner and wipe the needle with it as shown in fig. 2-16. Pull the needle through the towel while rotating it until it's clean. (Never push it—you could poke yourself or damage the tip.)

To keep paint from sticking to the needle, put a few drops of light oil (such as LaBelle no. 108 or Badger "Regdab" no. 122) on a paper towel and pull the needle through it. Doing this periodically will keep your airbrush operating smoothly.

Airbrush capacity

Airbrush tips are generally available with openings in three sizes: small, medium, and large. Model railroaders do nearly all their work with the large tip. The small and medium tips are designed for spraying inks and very thin paints. They're usually used by artists and others who need to sometimes paint in pencil-thin lines.

Our cousins in the model plane and car hobbies sometimes use these fine tips for free-handing designs like camouflage or racing stripes, whereas model railroaders generally use airbrushes like miniature spray guns. Feel free to experiment and play with them, however—you never know when the appropriate moment may arise to use them. Using smaller tips with model paints sometimes can result in clogged airbrushes and other problems.

Accessories

Figures 2-17 and 2-18 show some additional accessories and tools that you'll find handy. Paint jars in 1-ounce and ½-ounce sizes are nice for mixing paint and holding thinner. Glass eyedroppers and plastic siphon tubes (for water-based paints) are useful for transferring paint between bottles and measuring paint while mixing.

Keep plenty of paper towels, pipe cleaners, and cotton swabs handy for cleaning up.

Most airbrush kits include all the wrenches or tools needed to disassemble the airbrush. Keep these tools handy at your spray booth.

Now that you have the airbrush and other equipment figured out, let's move to Chapter 3 and put it to use.

Fig. 2-17. Bottles with graduation marks are handy for mixing paint, but a bit of masking tape also works well.

Fig. 2-18. If you spray paint straight from bottles, using a filter will reduce the chances of getting a blob of unmixed paint stuck in your airbrush.

3 Painting Techniques

Using airbrushes and brushes to create smooth finish coats on models

Along with painting itself, there are many other techniques to learn before you can paint a model: preparing the model, masking, adding decals, and cleaning up. Sometimes it seems as though the painting is the quick and easy part, while all the other related tasks consume the most time.

Fig. 3-1. It's important to wash models to remove fingerprints, oil, and mold-release compounds.

Preparing models for painting

Regardless of the brand or type of paint you're using, it's important that your model's surfaces are clean and free of dust, oil, grease, and other unwanted materials. Plastic models often have residue from mold-release agents, and brass models may have oil or residue from soldering flux. If you've handled the models at all, you've left fingerprints of oil from your skin, as shown in fig. 3-1. Any of these conditions can keep paint from sticking or result in an uneven paint surface.

Types of plastic

The most common plastics used in modeling are polystyrene (usually called styrene), ABS (acrylic butyl styrene), and various brands of slippery engineering plastic, such as Delrin.

Most plastic locomotive and freight car shells, building kits, details, and scratchbuilding materials are styrene. Some detail parts and scratchbuilding materials (notably those made by Plastruct) are ABS. Engineering plastic is generally used for items with moving joints, such as truck sideframes, or parts that are sprung—especially those with small cross sections, such as handrails.

Styrene generally takes paint well, although there are hundreds of varieties. Styrene from different manufacturers can vary in its characteristics. Manufacturers may use different types of styrene, or they may use varying amounts of recycled material and other additives. Some types of styrene are softer and less expensive to produce, but they are more susceptible to damage by lacquers and various solvents.

Painting ABS can be challenging because it is oilier than styrene. Delrin and other engineering plastics are the toughest of all to paint because their "self-lubricating" quality—which makes them ideal for trucks and other applications involving friction—means that paint doesn't stick very well to them. Also, since these parts are often quite flexible, paint must flex with the part or it will crack and peel off.

I've had good luck painting engineering plastic with Accu-Flex, which lives up to its name—it's very flexible. Flex additives can be added to other paints. Check auto paint shops for them—Morton no. 200-8 "Impact Coating" is one—and follow the directions on the product.

Preparing plastic

To clean a plastic model, use a soft-bristle toothbrush to scrub its surface with dish detergent and water. Be sure to scrub all the nooks and crannies of the model, including the grills and ladders. Don't use liquid soap—it will leave a film behind. Don't use alcohol ("rubbing" or denatured) to clean plastic, either. Many types of rubbing alcohol leave behind a film when they evaporate, and alcohol draws oil to the surface of plastic.

When you're finished scrubbing, rinse the model with plenty of warm water to make sure that all of the detergent is gone. From this point on, don't use your fingers to handle the model. Wear a pair of latex rubber gloves and handle the model carefully. To keep water spots from forming on the surface, use an airbrush (without paint) to blow the water away. Place the model in a dust-free area (in a cabinet or box) and allow it to dry completely.

Brass

Painting brass models can be just as challenging as painting plastic. Contrary to belief, lacquers don't grip brass any better than acrylics. The most important element in each paint is the resin. Most model paints stick well to brass, provided you've done a good job of preparing the surface.

If you're painting a commercial brass model, such as a locomotive or freight car, check to see if the model's surface is raw brass or if it has been given a clear coat at the factory. Most brass manufacturers give their models a clear-coat finish to keep the brass from tarnishing.

If this is the case, you have two options: paint over the clear coat or strip the clear finish and paint on the brass itself. In general, if the clear coat is thin, applied evenly, and is smooth, with no chips, drips, runs, or blobs, it's best to paint over it. The clear coat then serves as a primer for the following coats of paint.

If there are imperfections on the finish, or if the clear coat flakes off when you rub or scratch it with a fingernail, the finish must be stripped.

Stripping brass

To strip a brass model, separate it into subassemblies and make sure that any plastic parts are removed. Submerge the model in lacquer thinner until you see the finish blister on the surface. Do this outside or in a vented spray booth. Wearing chemical-resistant gloves, use a wood-handled brush to scrub the model until the finish is gone.

This can be a messy process, and sometimes the finish will stick remarkably well to the surface (which is why it's wise to strip the clear coat only if absolutely necessary). If the lacquer thinner doesn't completely remove the paint, try a bath in acetone instead.

An ultrasonic cleaner is a handy tool if you have access to one. Place the model in a diluted ammonia solution (or the cleaning solution recommended by the manufacturer) and the cleaner will often free any remaining paint or finish stuck in cracks and crevices. Another way to remove the clear finish (or any paint job) from brass is with a benchtop sandblasting unit, as in fig. 3-2.

Brass often tarnishes over time, and the tarnish should be removed before painting. To do this, brush a solution of DuPont Metal Prep (item no. VM-5717) onto the surface and rinse it with distilled water (be sure to follow the manufacturer's safety instructions carefully). Copper cleansers, such as Cameo, also work.

Now the preparation is the same as for plastic. Give the model a good scrubbing with detergent and a toothbrush, then rinse and dry it. Don't rely solely on a lacquer-thinner rinse to prepare the brass surface.

Some modelers take an additional step to prepare their models by etching the brass surface. Be careful to etch only raw brass—don't do it on brass with a coat of clear finish. Etching can be done with an air-abrasive unit or by soaking a model in white vinegar for about 20 minutes. The goal is to etch the surface lightly, giving the paint some "tooth" to hold on to. After soaking the model, follow with a detergent wash as described above.

Chapters 10 and 11 show brass painting projects from start to finish.

Polyester resin

Many limited-run and craftsman rolling stock and craftsman kits are cast in some type of polyester or urethane resin. These can be prepared the same way as plastic. Many of these materials have a very slippery surface, so it's extremely important to clean the surface before painting.

Wood

Wood usually holds paint well. A problem with models is that the grain sometimes shows through the paint when you don't want it to. To prevent this from occurring, use a primer with filler (such as Floquil's gray Primer) or a sanding sealer before adding the finish color.

Don't wash wood to clean it, and don't paint it if it's wet. Use a soft brush to sweep away sawdust and other materials that could interfere with paint.

Plaster

There are several nice structure kits and detail parts molded in Hydrocal and other types of plaster. Since it's a very porous material, plaster not only holds paint well—it almost drinks it in! Because plaster absorbs paint very quickly, it can be difficult to apply an even color coat with a brush. It can also require a lot of paint.

To alleviate these problems, spray the plaster with a light coat of clear finish or primer. This will help seal the surface and make it easier to paint.

If you're using plaster castings to represent various types of stone and block material, take advantage of plaster's porous quality to give individual blocks highlights by applying paint in washes. For some great tips on painting plaster, read *Realistic Model Railroad Scenery* by Dave Frary.

Airbrushing

Mixing paint

Some paints are ready for spraying straight from the bottle, but most must be thinned. Fig. 3-3 lists model paints and the manufacturers' suggested thinning ratios for each. It's a good idea to

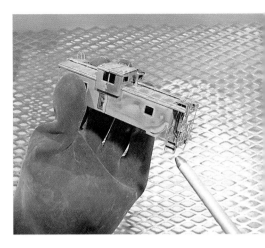

Fig. 3-2. A benchtop sandblaster like this one from North Coast Prototype Models works well to strip paint and etch brass.

use these as a starting point, then adjust the mixtures to suit your requirements. Paints act differently depending upon conditions such as temperature and humidity.

As I mentioned in Chapter 1, each of these paints uses a different resin and a different type of thinner. Using a thinner not designed for a paint can cause paints to gum up, limit their adhesion, or create other problems. For the same reason, never mix different brands of paint.

Floquil warrants a special mention. Until 1991, Floquil's Railroad Colors line, with Dio-Sol as a thinner, could cause styrene to craze. Bottles of this paint can be identified by solid red labels. In 1991, Floquil changed the formula of this paint to make it compatible with most plastics. Labels on these paints have black-and-red labels. The company also introduced Floquil Airbrush Thinner, which is safe to use on most plastics. The old- and new-formula paints may be mixed, and the new-formula paints can still be used with Dio-Sol, but in both cases the resulting mixture may not be plastic-compatible.

Solvent-based paints, such as Floquil's pre-1991 formula and Scalecoat, sometimes craze polystyrene plastics. However, this usually isn't a problem when you're airbrushing because the paint dries before it can do any harm. In fact, it can be beneficial, as the reacting paint will etch the surface just enough to get a good grip and improve adhesion.

Both Floquil and Scalecoat make coatings to protect against crazing: Floquil Barrier and Scalecoat Shieldcoat. Using them will prevent damage to your model, but in effect they add an extra (potentially detail-hiding) layer of paint. If you're uncomfortable about using these paints on plastics, try an acrylic instead.

It's a good idea to mix paints for airbrushing in a separate bottle. Floquil makes 1- and ½-ounce bottles, and other companies make similar ones. Be sure to label each bottle and include the date it was mixed.

Only mix as much as you think you'll use in a session, as some paints separate over time (especially if you've added 40 to 50 percent thinner) because thinning changes the balance of resin and solvents.

If you're painting a multicolor scheme in which one color will be applied over another, it's wise to use the same brand of paint for each color. It's often possible to paint one brand or type of paint on top of another without adverse reactions, provided that the first paint layer has fully cured (for least a week). Test the paint compatibility on scrap material before trying it on your model.

Firing up the airbrush

You're finally ready to start painting. Begin by practicing on some plain white cardboard and old model shells (I recommend visiting a swap meet and buying a handful of broken 75-cent freight cars). Turn on your air supply and adjust it to the desired pressure, then add the paint to the airbrush.

Start with the nozzle closed, then push the trigger and gradually open the nozzle until you get a smooth flow of paint. Figure 3-4 shows the basic airbrushing stroke. Begin spraying to one side of the model, move it steadily across the surface, and continue spraying until the airbrush is well past the model.

If you make a "U-turn" while the airbrush is still over the model, the result will be a thick application of

Fig. 3-3

Paint	Solvent or water base	Safe to brush on bare plastic?	Thinner	Airbrush dilution	Spray pressure (psi)	Cleanup
Accu-Flex	Water	Yes	Water	Usually not necessary	32–35	Water
Accu-paint	Solvent	No	AP-100 thinner	75% paint, 25% thinner	15–20	Lacquer thinner
Floquil Railroad (black-and-red label) and Military Colors	Solvent	Yes	Floquil Airbrush Thinner	Gloss: 50% paint, 50% thinner; Flat: 75% paint, 25% thinner	12–20	Lacquer thinner
Floquil Railroad Colors, pre-1991 formula (all-red label)	Solvent	No	Dio-Sol	75% paint, 20% thinner, 5% Glaze	12–20	Lacquer thinner
Pactra Acrylic Enamel	Water	Yes	Denatured alcohol	65% paint, 35% thinner	25	Water
Polly S	Water	Yes	Polly S Airbrush thinner	60% paint, 40% thinner	25	Water
Polly Scale	Water	Yes	Polly S Airbrush thinner	75% paint 25% thinner	20–30	Water
Pro Color	Water	Yes	Water	90% paint, 10% thinner	25–30	Water
Scalecoat	Solvent	No	Scalecoat Thinner	50% paint, 50% thinner	15–20	Lacquer thinner
Scalecoat II	Solvent	Yes	Scalecoat II Thinner	50% paint, 50% thinner	15–20	Lacquer thinner
Testor's Dullcote and Glosscote	Solvent	No	Lacquer thinner	50% paint, 50% thinner	20–25	Lacquer thinner

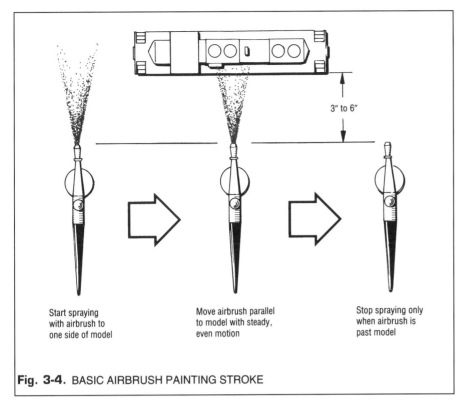

Start spraying with airbrush to one side of model

Move airbrush parallel to model with steady, even motion

Stop spraying only when airbrush is past model

3" to 6"

Fig. 3-4. BASIC AIRBRUSH PAINTING STROKE

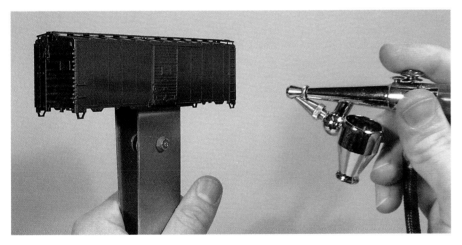

Fig. 3-5. Accu-Flex Dark Tuscan Oxide Red covers well. Note that the paint is wet immediately after hitting the body, but the paint at left (at the beginning of the stroke) is already drying.

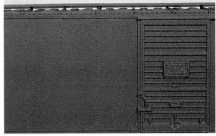

Fig. 3-6. The color and sheen should be even across the surface. Tiny details like rivets should stand out, with no signs of the paint pooling in recesses or around raised details.

Use back-and-forth strokes, each slightly overlapping the previous one, until the surface is covered. As soon as the paint dries, you're ready to apply the second coat—usually, by the time you've given each side of a model one coat, the first side will be ready for the second.

As you apply the second coat, adjust your spraying angle to cover all sides of details such as ladders and grills. Be sure to get into corners. Each additional coat of paint can cover details, so never use more paint than you have to. Figure 3-6 shows the results.

Frequently check the model under a bright light. The color should be even throughout, with no signs of the underlying color. You shouldn't be able to see signs of your spray pattern, and the sheen should be uniform. When you're satisfied, set the model aside in a dust-free area to dry.

Each brand and type of paint behaves differently, so test the paint before using it on a "real" model. Experiment until you find the right combination of pressure, dilution, spraying distance, and amount of paint (controlled by adjusting the color control tip or needle). Here are some possible solutions to problems that can arise:

• **Paint dries before hitting model**—pressure too high; spraying distance too far from model; not enough paint coming through brush.

• **Paint stays wet too long on model or paint runs**—spraying distance too close to model; too much paint coming through airbrush; paint diluted too much; not moving airbrush quickly enough across surface.

paint where you reversed your stroke.

Most airbrush painting errors are a result of a stationary airbrush. Remember that the airbrush should always be moving when the trigger is down.

You're looking for a paint coat like the one in fig. 3-5—heavy enough that the surface is covered, but not so heavy that the paint pools or runs. The paint should be wet when it hits the surface, but should dry quickly. The difference is easy to see with flat and semigloss paints, but can be difficult to see with gloss colors.

Figure 3-5 shows a paint that covers well. With some lighter colors, the model surface will show through the first coat. Don't worry about it—the surface will be covered by succeeding coats. If you try to apply too much paint at once, runs or waves will appear in the paint finish.

A spray pattern that's too light can also cause problems, such as a pebbly, grainy, uneven finish. If the paint is dry when it hits the model or dries too quickly, the paint won't adhere well to the surface.

- **Paint not covering well**—paint diluted too much.
- **Paint spatters or airbrush clogs**—pressure too low; paint not mixed well or not sufficiently diluted; paint buildup on airbrush tip; dirty airbrush, control tip, or siphon tube; bent needle or control-tip cone.
- **Paint coverage uneven**—airbrush strokes not smooth; airbrush stopping before edge of model; inconsistent spraying distance from model.
- **Paint doesn't dry or stays tacky on model**—paint not mixed sufficiently; incompatible paint-thinner mix; reaction between solvent and surface.
- **Paint cracks while drying**—paint applied too heavily and is drying unevenly; second layer of paint incompatible with first layer.
- **Acrylic paint pulls away from some areas on surface**—surface not clean: oils are repelling paint.

If you paint continuously for more than a minute or two, you may notice a reduction in the amount of paint emitted by the airbrush. This is caused by paint drying on the airbrush tip. Aim the airbrush away from the model, depress the trigger, and open up the nozzle a bit more. If it happens again, use a corner of a paper towel dipped in thinner to clean off the tip. If you don't clean it periodically, you risk having a blotch of paint fly out and hit the model.

Fixing problems

If a bit of paint splatters on your model, don't panic. First, inspect your airbrush and fix what caused the problem so it doesn't happen again. Little imperfections like this often aren't noticeable on a finished model, particularly one that you're planning to weather.

If the splatter is standing in the way of a smooth finish and you need to remove it, let the paint fully cure. Use a bit of fine (600-grit) sandpaper and carefully sand down the offending bit of paint. Wash the model, add another coat of paint, and the damage should be hidden.

Runs are a bit more serious. Immediately after one appears, back the airbrush away from the model and

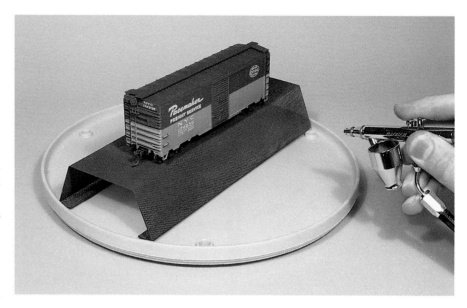

Fig. 3-7. An inexpensive lazy susan, with a paint stand on top of it, makes it easy to turn models. Here I'm applying a weathering spray to a boxcar featured in Chapter 8.

quickly spray air (without paint) at the run to level it as much as possible. Direct the run away from any fine details. If the run is still too apparent once it dries, wait until the paint is cured and sand it down as described previously. Use the same technique to eliminate fingerprints.

If paint cracks or if the paint finish is grainy (the paint was dry when hitting the surface) there's little you can do but strip the model and repaint. This is also sometimes the best approach for serious runs that have trailed into a detailed area.

Holding models for airbrushing

A painting handle from GB Engineering, shown in fig. 3-5, is a handy tool for holding locomotive and car shells. You can also use cardboard tubes and blocks of wood. Small items can be taped to a piece of cardboard or held with tweezers or pliers.

An inexpensive lazy susan placed in a spray booth, as in fig. 3-7, makes it easy to turn items around while painting without handling them.

Baking paint

To speed drying time and get a tougher paint finish, many modelers use heat to bake the paint on their brass and other

all-metal models. Although it isn't necessary, baking speeds the curing time and results in a harder, tougher paint finish.

Since oven thermostats are notoriously inaccurate, place a thermometer in the oven to check the temperature. After applying each color, bake the model at about 175 degrees Fahrenheit for one hour. Some solders have relatively low melting points, so higher temperatures may leave you with a partially disassembled mess in your oven.

Hair dryers are handy for drying acrylic paints on plastic models. Keep the dryer moving over the entire model for a minute. With many acrylics, such as Accu-Flex, this is enough to cure the paint and allow you to immediately apply decals or the next paint color.

Clear overcoats

Besides using clear coats to provide a uniform sheen over an entire model, modelers frequently use them to provide a gloss surface for decals and to seal lettering and weathering. Several companies make clear gloss, satin (semigloss), and flat finishes.

Apply clear finishes with an airbrush if at all possible. It's difficult to achieve an even finish with a spray can or brush. The best flat finish I've found is Testor's Dullcote, mixed 1:1 with lacquer thinner and applied with an airbrush. For a high-gloss finish, try

Removing paint
Fixing mistakes and renovating old models

Every once in a while something goes wrong while you're painting—the paint runs, goes on dry and doesn't hold properly, acquires fingerprints, or just isn't what you were hoping for. It's a disappointing feeling, and the first temptation can be to throw the model away and pack up the airbrush.

If this happens, don't panic—and don't let anger take over. A commercial paint remover will usually get you back to where you started. It's important to remove the paint as soon as possible, because if you can do it before the paint fully cures it will come off easily.

Stick with commercial paint removers—Polly S ELO and Scalecoat Paint Remover are two popular solutions. Don't use brake fluid, as most brands in use today are synthetic and won't do a good job. It's also hazardous to handle and difficult to remove.

Over the years modelers have used other products such as Pine-Sol and oven cleaner. I don't recommend them, because most are hazardous and all can attack and craze plastic. I recently found an engine shell that I had stripped with Pine-Sol 18 years earlier—I could still smell the Pine-Sol!

Whichever remover you choose, if you're stripping plastic or resin, test it by applying a few drops inside the shell. Let this sit for 30 minutes, then wipe it off. There shouldn't be any sign of crazing.

Most paint removers recommend that you brush the solution on, wait for the paint to bubble, then wash it off. It may take a couple of applications to do the job. If the paint is still sticking, then you may have to submerge the model. Don't let the model sit in the remover for too long. As soon as the paint starts to bubble, pull out the model and use an old toothbrush to scrub it. Rinse the model under running water to remove the paint residue.

Stripping factory-painted models

It's always an adventure to remove paint from commercial models. Some paint almost falls off, while other paint simply won't come off. Use the same techniques as I described above.

To save yourself the hassle and expense of stripping models, if at all possible, purchase an undecorated model.

If the factory paint is applied in a thin layer, you can usually get good results by stripping only the lettering. Chapter 4 explains how to do this. Look for single-color models with thin coats of paint.

Begin by brushing paint remover on the surface. Let it sit until the paint starts to bubble, then scrub it off and rinse it with water. If the paint hasn't cured, it will usually come off quite easily.

ABOVE LEFT: You never know what might be lurking beneath a coat of paint. Under its black paint this tender, from a locomotive purchased at a swap meet, once wore a Burlington Northern green scheme, which had been applied over the original factory black scheme. Since this paint was holding the model very well, immersion was the only way to strip it (this is Polly S ELO). **ABOVE RIGHT:** Two hours of soaking and a great deal of scrubbing removed most of the paint on the left side, although the line along the rivets will need more paint remover. This car illustrates why stripping old models or factory-painted models sometimes is not worth the effort.

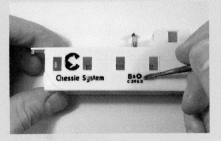 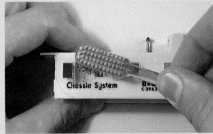

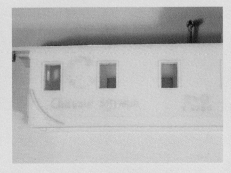

ABOVE LEFT: Sometimes you just need to remove the lettering before repainting a model. To do this, start by applying paint remover (ELO in this case) over the lettering. **ABOVE RIGHT:** Scrub the lettering with a toothbrush. **RIGHT:** Rinse off the lettering, then give the model a detergent-and-water scrubbing. The shell is now ready for a new coat of paint.

airbrushing Floquil Crystal Cote mixed 3:1 with Floquil Airbrush Thinner. For a semigloss sheen, mix Dullcote and Glosscote 1:1 and blend that with an equal part of lacquer thinner, or try Floquil Flat Finish mixed 3:1 with Floquil Airbrush Thinner.

The key to good results with any of these products is to apply them in thin coats. Never allow them to stay wet on a model for more than a second. Three thin coats are always better than one heavy one.

If you don't own an airbrush, I'd suggest using Model Master Semi-gloss Clear Lacquer from a spray can. Apply this in very light coats. For brushing, try Accu-Flex Clear Flat, Clear Satin, and Clear Gloss.

Be sure that any clear finish you apply does not change the color of the underlying paint. Some clear finishes actually have a light amber color. It's always a good idea to test a clear finish on scrap material before using it on a prized model.

It's usually safe to apply clear finishes over paint of a different brand, provided you use thin coats and the base coat has fully cured. If you have any doubts, test first.

Clear-coat problems

Occasionally clear coats applied using an airbrush will fog or get cloudy as they dry on a model. Water-based flats are the most susceptible, and the most likely causes are paint that wasn't sufficiently mixed or was applied too heavily. With an acrylic, you can usually strip the clear finish with denatured alcohol. Do this as soon as possible, before the clear coat has a chance to fully cure. This will also remove any decals, but should leave the underlying paint alone, provided that it has fully cured.

Another option is to apply a lacquer gloss coat over the cloudy water-based finish. This will often make the clouded areas disappear. If this doesn't work and the cloudy areas reappear as the lacquer dries, give the model a bath in denatured alcohol to strip both clear coats. If neither technique works, the only solution is to strip the model, including paint.

If a lacquer clear coat turns cloudy, chances are it was applied too heavily and has etched the underlying paint. (This is why it's important to apply clear finishes in thin coats.) If this is the case, strip the model and start over.

Note: When working with denatured alcohol, take the same precautions as when working with paint solvents. Work outdoors or in a vented spray booth.

Aerosol cans

If you don't own an airbrush, spray cans can still give you a good paint finish. If you're interested in saving money, though, remember that for the amount of paint you get, spray cans are fairly expensive. If you do a lot of painting, investing in an airbrush and air supply will pay for itself over time.

Using spray cans requires the same precautions as airbrushing lacquers: Use them outdoors or in a vented spray booth, and wear a respirator.

Spray cans limit your control of both the pressure and the amount of paint—when you push the nozzle, you get what comes out. Paint usually comes out too fast and heavy, so it's important to keep the can moving. Hold the aerosol cans about 12" away from the model surface, as opposed to 2" to 5" for airbrushing. Be sure to test before working on a model.

Paint from an aerosol can takes longer to dry than the paint that's been airbrushed. You'll want to make the initial coat very light and wait about 20 minutes before adding succeeding coats.

Fig. 3-8. If an aerosol can gets plugged, pull off the nozzle and free the clog with a pin.

It can also take more coats to cover, since the paint in spray cans must be thinned quite a bit to make it flow freely. Wait at least 48 hours before masking and applying a second color.

When you've finished spraying, hold the can upside down and push the nozzle until there is no more paint coming out. This will clear paint from the nozzle and keep it from clogging. If a nozzle clogs, pull it off the can as shown in fig. 3-8 and use a straight pin to clear out the nozzle at the base.

Aerosol cans work best when they're warm, 70 degrees or above. If you're painting in a cool area, warm the can by setting it in a jar of warm (not hot) water for half an hour before spraying.

Two disadvantages of spray cans are that there aren't as many colors available as there are in bottles, and that it's impossible to mix your own colors. However, Floquil, Pactra, and Testor all have a wide range of colors in spray paints.

You can find many other brands of paint, in many colors, at hardware and paint stores. These can be handy, but pigments in many of these paints aren't ground as fine as in model paints. Many will cover in thick coats, which will obscure details on models. Be sure to test them before using them on a model.

Brush-painting

Painting a finish by brush is largely a lost art, mainly because it's impossible to obtain as thin and smooth a finish as with an airbrush. However, brush-painting still has many devotees, some out of necessity. With some practice, it's possible to give a model an even coat of paint with a brush.

Don't skimp on the quality of your brushes. You don't need to spend a fortune on them, but avoid the 10-for-89-cent variety. Figure 3-9 shows several that I keep handy. I keep separate brushes for light and dark colors.

Soft brushes, such as the Floquil no. 3 pure sable, are great for finish painting. The larger brush sizes hold quite a bit of paint, and the soft bristles leave a smooth finish with a minimum of visible brush strokes.

To paint a model with a brush, use as wide a brush as practical. The no. 3

works well for most HO scale applications. Dip the bristles in the paint (only submerge the lower third of the bristles) and brush the paint on the surface as in fig. 3-10. Use as few strokes as possible—the paint will level itself. If you continue to brush the paint as it dries, you'll leave brush strokes that will dry in place. On the car shown I was able to get from one edge of each surface to the other with single strokes.

Keeping your strokes parallel, add another brushful of paint to an adjoining area. Brush in a direction that matches surface details and lines. On freight cars and locomotives, keep your strokes vertical—the direction that weathering naturally occurs. That way if any brush strokes appear, they'll look like light weathering.

Continue brushing until the area is covered. Wait until the paint is thoroughly dry before adding another coat. Figure 3-11 shows the finished car.

One disadvantage of brush painting is that the coats of paint are heavier than with airbrushing. Another disadvantage is that it's difficult to get light colors (especially yellows) to cover well. It's important to provide an even undercoat (such as light gray) to ensure good coverage for a final light coat.

Brush-painting details

Brush-painting is especially valuable in working with details. Several chapters in this book show how brush-painting can be used to create various effects.

Synthetic brushes are good for pinpoint work, since they hold their shape and their fine points well, but solvent-based paints can damage them. My favorite fine-point synthetic is the Testor's Model Master no. 0 in fig. 3-9. Note how this brush has a much finer point than the no. 0 sable next to it.

For painting details with solvent-based paints, I like Floquil 3/0 (three-ought) and 5-0 pure sables. They have fine points, but won't hold as much paint as the no. 0 brush. Flat, wide brushes, like the ½" sable and ox-hair brushes shown, are good for applying washes. They're also useful for painting finish colors over large, even surfaces.

Fig. 3-9. From the top: Floquil 5/0 pure sable; Testor's Model Master no. 0 synthetic; Floquil nos. 0 and 2 sables; Floquil no. 3 pure sable; Model Master ½" flat black sable; and Floquil ½" flat ox hair.

Fig. 3-10. Flow the paint onto the surface with as few brush strokes as possible. This is a Floquil no. 3 pure sable and Accu-Flex Dark Tuscan Oxide Red paint straight from the bottle.

Fig. 3-11. Two coats covered the black styrene nicely. If you look really close you'll see some brush marks, but with care brush-painting can produce a very nice finish.

23

Cleaning brushes

Clean brushes are vital to obtaining good results. Traces of dried paint on a brush can result in color bleed or small particles being transferred to a model.

To clean a brush, swish it around in a jar of thinner (water for acrylics; lacquer thinner for solvent-based paints), then pull the brush out, drain the excess thinner against the lip of the bottle, and wipe the brush on a paper towel. Repeat this until all traces of the paint are gone from the brush.

When you're using acrylics, clean the brushes under running water, if possible, while working the bristles gently with your fingers to remove paint. Add a drop of dish detergent to the brush, work it in with your fingers, and rinse it again with running water.

When the brush is clean, and while the bristles are still wet, reform the brush tip to its proper shape. When using acrylic paints it's important to wet the brush before using it and to clean the brush frequently as you're using it. This helps keep paint from drying on the bristles. Once acrylics dry, water no longer dissolves the paint.

Leaving a brush in paint thinner or jabbing the brush tip against the bottom of the container can destroy the shape of the bristles.

Store your brushes with bristles up. I use an old plastic drinking cup, with the lip of the cup below the bristles. If the bristles are allowed to rest on the side of the cup, they can take on a new shape.

Keeping paint fresh

Air is the number one enemy of paint. As soon as you open a jar, the paint begins to dry. Keep lids on paint bottles as much as possible. If you're brush-painting a model and will be working on it for more than a couple of minutes, don't leave the jar open. Instead, put an eyedropper of paint in a holding cup or separate bottle.

Keep your bottles clean. Wipe off the bottle and cap threads before replacing the cap. This will make it easier to open the jar the next time, and it will also ensure a more airtight seal on the bottle. If you wipe a bit of Vaseline on the jar threads when you first open a jar it will be easier to clean off later and will make the cap easier to remove and seal.

When you open a jar of acrylic paint, you may sometimes find a blob of rubbery paint near the seal. Peel it away and discard it to make sure it doesn't get mixed in with the paint (and gum up your airbrush).

Masking

When painting a model with two colors, it's necessary to cover one color with tape or other material. Modelers need something that leaves a clean, sharp edge and is flexible enough to go around details. The tape should be sticky enough to hold firmly to the underlying paint so that the second color won't bleed underneath it; however it must not take paint with it when it's removed, and it shouldn't leave any residue behind.

Modelers use a wide variety of tapes for masking. You'll find modelers who swear by their type of tape, but I've seen contest-quality models done with each.

Standard masking tape is probably the most used, and is what I prefer to use. The fact that it is quite tacky (meaning it's more likely to pull up underlying paint) and it lacks sharp edges are clear disadvantages to using masking tape. However, you can fix this by pressing a strip firmly on a piece of glass and cutting a new edge with a sharp hobby knife. The cut edge will leave a clean paint line, and the action of applying and removing the tape will decrease its tackiness.

However, if you're having recurring problems pulling off underlying paint, chances are that it's not the paint—it's more likely that the surface wasn't sufficiently clean or the first coat of paint hasn't cured properly.

Drafting tape looks like masking tape, but its glue isn't nearly as tacky. Many modelers prefer it because it's less likely to remove previous layers of paint. However, I've found it to be not tacky enough—it sometimes doesn't stay put, and it can peel up after being applied on a model, resulting in paint bleeding under the edge. If you use it, be sure to cut a clean edge, as with masking tape.

Many modelers have success using Scotch Magic Transparent tape. It has a sharp, clean edge, and the tackiness of the glue is about right. However, it's not very flexible and can be difficult to work around rivet lines, doors, and other details.

Badger Photo Frisket is a very thin, clear plastic material with a peel-off adhesive back. It comes in 8½" x 11" sheets, and cuts easily with a knife or small scissors. It leaves a good, sharp line, but it's not very flexible, making it suitable for flat surfaces only.

Masking solutions such as Microscale Micro Mask and Walthers Magic Mask are liquid rubber materials that you can apply with a brush. They peel away after they dry. They're handy for masking around small details, corners, axle ends, and other odd areas.

It's always wise to use as little tape on a model as possible to reduce the chance of lifting paint. If you're covering a large area, use tape around the edges and paper over the rest.

Chapters 8-11 include various techniques for masking and applying more than one color.

A couple of additional masking tips:

• Spray the second color as soon as possible after applying the masking. Avoid aiming the airbrush toward the edge of the tape. If you're brush-painting, don't slop paint over the tape edge. Instead, work the paint carefully to the mask line.

• Remove the tape as soon as possible when you've finished painting. The longer that masking tape sits on a model, the more likely it is to leave residue behind.

• When removing tape, pull it back across itself at a sharp angle. Taking it off this way reduces the stress on the underlying paint.

• If some of the second color creeps under the mask, use a small brush to touch up the areas. If a large area is affected, wait until the final coat has cured, mask it off, and airbrush the first color over the area.

Congratulations! You're now ready to add lettering to the beautiful paint finish you've created.

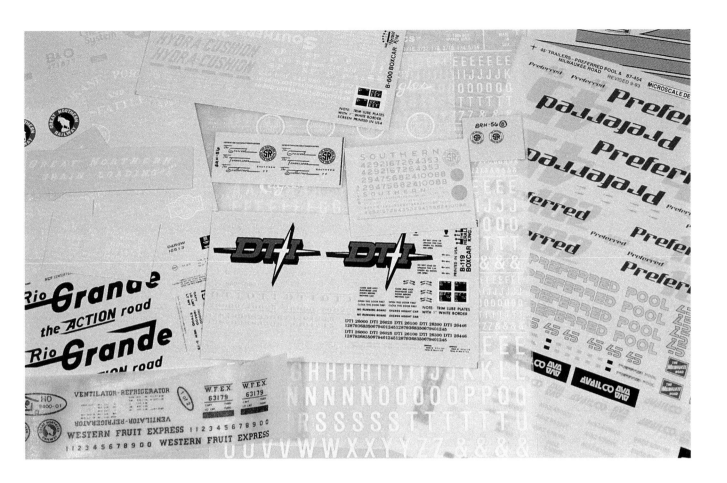

4 Decals and Dry Transfers

Achieving a painted-on look with lettering and designs

Now that you have a model with a nice paint job, the next step is to add lettering. Decals and dry transfers make models come alive. By duplicating the lettering and herald styles of prototype equipment, your models will begin to look much more realistic.

Decals (wet transfers) and dry transfers are available from many sources. Larger companies such as Champion, Herald King, Microscale, and CDS offer hundreds of lettering sets covering railroads and private owners across the country. In addition, dozens of smaller companies and individuals offer lettering sets for a few railroads or types of equipment.

Decals and dry transfers each have advantages and disadvantages, and you'll find modelers who swear by each method. When used properly, either will do a fine job of re-creating lettering in miniature.

Decals

These transfers have ink on a clear film attached to a paper backing. The backing releases when you soak the decal in water. The clear film is then applied to the model.

It's important to apply decals to a gloss or semigloss surface. Decals will not adhere to coarse surfaces, such as flat paint.

Fig. 4-1 shows how trapped air under the decal results in a silvered appearance, which is compounded if you apply a clear flat finish over the decal. Consequently, you must either paint models with gloss or semigloss paints, or coat flat paints with clear gloss finishes prior to decaling.

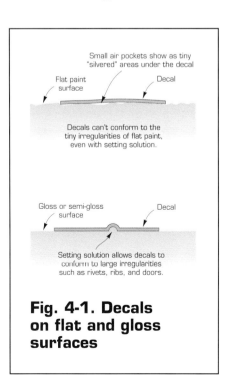

Small air pockets show as tiny "silvered" areas under the decal

Flat paint surface

Decal

Decals can't conform to the tiny irregularities of flat paint, even with setting solution.

Gloss or semi-gloss surface

Decal

Setting solution allows decals to conform to large irregularities such as rivets, ribs, and doors.

Fig. 4-1. Decals on flat and gloss surfaces

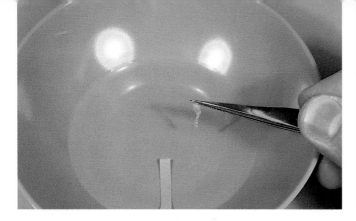

Fig. 4-2. Sometimes decals that have floated off the backing paper twist and curl when you remove them from water.

Fig. 4-3. Set them back in the water, then use tweezers to grab the backing paper and lift the decal from the water.

The manufacturers' directions provide the best instructions for handling and applying the various types of decals. The main difference among decals is the thickness of the film. Some brands, such as Microscale, use a very thin film. As the Microscale directions state, dip the decal in water for a few seconds, then place it on a towel for approximately one minute. Slide the decal directly from the backing paper to the model. If you allow large decals to float in the water, they may fold over onto themselves when you try to pick them up, as shown in figs. 4-2 and 4-3.

The film on Microscale decals doesn't cover the entire sheet—the film is only located under the image. The edges of the film are beveled slightly, which helps the decal blend in with the surface of the model. Don't trim off this outside edge if you can avoid it.

Other brands, such as Champion, use a thicker film. You can allow these decals to soak in the water until the backing paper releases. As the decal floats by itself on the water, most of the decal glue will disappear. Use tweezers to move the decal from the water to the model. For a large decal, slide the decal off the backing paper, just as you would with a thin-film decal.

The film on most of these decals covers the entire sheet. It's best to cut the decal close to the lettering or design to help hide the edge of the film.

A word on water

One of the best tips I know is to use distilled water for applying decals. The water at my home is so hard, it was leaving large water spots around decals.

Once I began using distilled water my models were much cleaner after the decals dried.

It's also a good idea to use only distilled water for thinning acrylic paint. Chemicals, minerals, bacteria, and other impurities in tap water can cause paint to do strange things. Distilled water is cheap, less than a buck a gallon, which is a small price to pay for better results.

Setting solutions

When decals were introduced, they used thick transfer films and included a healthy coating of adhesive. It was important to use plenty of adhesive on decals so that they would stick to the model. Unfortunately, the film and adhesive stood out prominently on models and were difficult to hide.

Decal-setting solutions have eliminated the need for that adhesive, other than to hold the decal to the backing paper until it's wet. Setting solutions effectively "melt" the decal film to the model. This makes decals conform to details such as rivets, door latches, weld seams, and corrugations, giving lettering and striping a painted-on look.

Setting solutions come in various strengths to match the characteristics of different manufacturers' decals. In general, it's a good idea to use the solution recommended by each manufacturer. Using too much fluid or using a strong solution on a thin decal film can cause ink to run and make decals sag and twist.

Microscale makes a pair of solutions, Micro Set and Micro Sol. Micro Set is the weaker of the two. If you apply it to a model's surface before positioning

a decal, you can still move the decal without damaging it. Once you position the decal for good, apply Micro Sol to melt it into place.

Other popular solutions, Walthers Solvaset and Champion Decal Set, are designed for thicker, tougher decals. Apply them only after the decal is in position. You can thin both of these products with distilled water to create weaker solutions.

Once you've applied setting solution, don't touch the decal until it's completely dry. As the solution works, the decal may wrinkle and appear distorted. Resist the temptation to try to "fix" it, because as it dries it will straighten itself out.

Residue from excess decal glue, setting solution, or water can sometimes leave a stain around the decal. After the decal has dried thoroughly, use a wet paintbrush to lightly scrub these areas clean.

Note that setting solutions occasionally craze paint if the paint hasn't fully cured. If you're concerned, test the solution on an obscure location before using it on decals. Also, don't flood the decal with solution—it's better to apply light coats two or three times than one heavy application.

Stripes

There are two schools of thought on applying decal stripes. One technique is to trim away all decal film except for the stripe. This eliminates any chance of seeing blank decal film on the model, but it can be tough to get a narrow stripe to behave. The other method is to trim the film as wide as

Applying Decals

Here are all the things you need to apply decals: freight car and decals (in this case an HO scale Walthers hopper car and Chicago, Burlington & Quincy decals from Kevin's Decals), a diagram of the car (included with the decals), hobby knife, straightedge (the clear triangle lets you see exactly where you're cutting), scale rule, fine-point tweezers, paper towel, setting solution, soft-bristle brushes, and foam (for sponging away dried glue residue). The magnifying lupe is handy for checking details close up and observing reference slides. The green self-healing mat is a handy cutting surface.

Begin by cutting the decal from the sheet. Because of the raised ribs on this car, you must apply each group of letters by itself.

Soak the decal in water to dissolve the adhesive. Let the decal soak in water for about 20 seconds, then remove it and set it on a paper towel for about 40 seconds. Use a small brush to slide the decal slowly from the paper to the model. You can also use tweezers as shown here, but be careful not to tear the decal.

Use a toothpick to position the decal on the model. Be sure to keep the decal wet. As you add each group of letters, sight down the car to make sure the lettering is straight. Press the corner of a paper towel on the edge of the decal to soak up excess water. Be careful not to move the decal.

Using a small brush, carefully apply decal-setting solution to the decal. Capillary action will pull the solution under the decal. Don't use a stroking motion—that could disturb the decal. Instead, dab the brush straight down, then lift it straight up.

When the decal is completely dry, slice any air bubbles with a sharp knife—don't let the knife gouge the model's surface—and then reapply setting solution.

Use a brush soaked in water to gently clean any decal glue or setting solution residue. If it still remains, use a bit of wet foam to gently scrub the area.

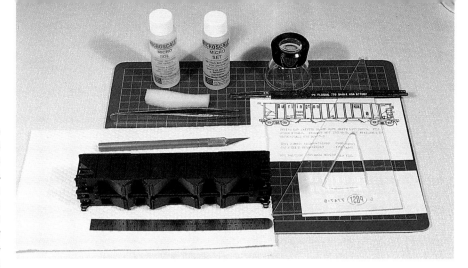

Once you've gathered all the essentials, you're ready to go.

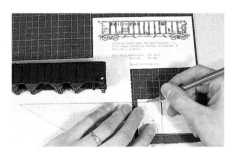

Step 1: Cut decal from the sheet.

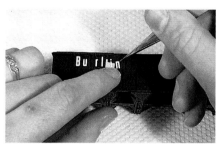

Step 2: Do long decals in sections.

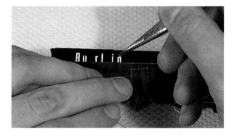

Step 3: Do a final decal positioning.

Step 4: Dab away excess water.

Step 5: Apply decal-setting solution.

Step 6: Slice out air bubbles.

The completed model

Fig. 4-4. Stripes on batten strips are among the toughest to apply.

Fig. 4-5. Start by sliding the stripe from the backing paper into place on the model.

Fig. 4-6. Use tweezers or the end of a toothpick to gently prod the decal into place, keeping the decal wet to prevent tearing it.

possible, with lots of blank decal film on either side of the stripe. This makes the stripe easier to apply and keep straight.

Since film is fairly easy to hide, I generally leave extra film when I'm applying a stripe on a large flat area. Sometimes, such as on a locomotive side sill, it's only possible to leave extra film on one edge of a stripe. If the stripe is going across a rough area where excess blank film will probably be noticed, then I trim the decal down to the stripe itself.

Figures 4-4, 4-5, and 4-6 show how to position stripes. The key is to take your time and make sure the stripe is straight. Keep the decal wet to make handling easier, and sight down the side of the model to keep things aligned. Don't apply setting solution until the stripe is exactly where you want it.

When working with long stripes, apply the stripe in several pieces. Apply one section at a time, and allow each section to dry for several minutes before applying the next. Then you won't accidentally knock a previously applied section out of alignment.

Saving old decals

Decals will usually last for years if they're kept in a dry, dark place. If they're kept out in the open or are exposed to bright light and humid conditions, they may become brittle, separate from the paper backing, or break apart when soaked in water.

You can save an old decal by brushing Microscale Micro Super Film over the surface, creating a new layer of clear film. When it dries, apply it like a regular decal.

Another way to save old decals is to give them a coat of clear gloss finish,

such as Floquil Crystal Cote. This will hold the decal together until you can get it on the model.

Fixing problems

Modelers sometimes worry about leaving decals in water for too long. However, if you forget about a decal and leave it floating in water for a few minutes—or even hours—don't worry. Just pick it out of the water with tweezers. Use a piece of paper to lift a large decal, as in figs. 4-2 and 4-3.

Once you apply the setting solution, how long do you have to correct a mistake, such as a misaligned decal, or worse, an incorrectly placed decal? In general, if you recognize your mistake within about 10 seconds after applying setting solution, you can flood the area with water from a brush and save the decal. After that, your only recourse is to blot up the melted decal and start over with a new one.

Occasionally a decal tears, usually because of a careless pull or twist. If you have a spare decal handy, it's wise to start over. However, it's possible to fix tears with no signs of damage.

If a decal is torn completely in two, apply the first part and set it with a small amount of setting solution. Once it dries, apply the second half in position against the first. Add more setting solution, and the decal should look as good as new.

When a decal is partially torn, you can float the entire thing into position using lots of water. Once it's in position, use the corner of a paper towel to remove most of the water. It's usually possible to get the decal in proper alignment unless the decal was twisted and pulled—in which case, a new decal is usually the best remedy.

Dry transfers

The main advantage of dry transfer (or "rub-on") lettering is that there's no decal film to hide—the lettering or design is the only element that stays on the model. Also, dry transfers go onto flat paint finishes just fine—there's no need to spray a gloss coating on a model before applying them, and no setting solution to use.

However, it can be difficult to apply dry transfers over irregular surfaces,

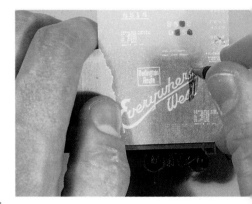

Fig. 4-7. Burnish the decal in one direction only until the design is transferred, then rub the paper in several directions.

Fig. 4-8. These HO scale dry transfers from CDS Lettering look almost painted on, down to the stencil breaks in the numbers and stripes.

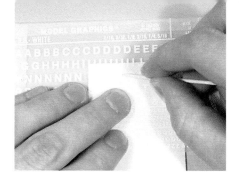

Fig. 4-9. Burnish dry transfers onto clear decal film, then add a clear gloss finish to seal them.

Fig. 4-10. Cut them from the film and apply them like regular decals.

Custom decals and dry transfers

Many modelers free-lance, or create their own fictitious railroads. If you are a free-lancer, custom decals with your railroad's herald help enhance the effect. Several companies will produce custom decals from artwork you provide, and other companies will prepare artwork for you.

You can also "steal" a herald or initials from a prototype railroad and create your own name using the initials or slogan of a prototype.

Several modelers have created believable model railroads by copying styles of prototype railroads as shown in fig. 4-11. "Borrowing" prototype

and small transfers can be tough to position and burnish.

It can be more difficult to align lettering and heralds on dry transfers. It may help to align the design if you trim the transfer sheet so that it's parallel with a line or edge on the model. Be sure to leave yourself enough material to hold on to.

Use a burnishing tool, rounded wood stick, or pencil or pen to rub the design into place, as shown in fig. 4-7. To avoid tearing the lettering, rub in one direction only until the design transfers to the surface. Once the design has transferred, finish burnishing by changing directions.

Be thorough, especially around rivets and other surface details. Use enough pressure to burnish the transfer, but don't use so much pressure that you create indentations on the surface or mar details. Figure 4-8 shows how dry transfers can appear to be painted on a model, with no decal film to hide.

Protecting lettering

Once your decals or dry transfers are in place, you want them to stay in place. Spraying the model with a coat of clear finish will help protect them and hide the edges. Don't overdo it—a thin coat is all you need. It's better to apply two thin coats than one heavy coat.

Creating special decals

If you can't find what you're looking for in a commercial set, don't give up. Most of the major decal and dry transfer manufacturers produce alphabet and number sets, stripes, shapes, stars, sheets of solid colors, plain decal film, and miscellaneous artwork. You can mix and match these to create

your own signs, roadnames, and heralds.

You can also make your own decals using dry transfers, as shown in figs. 4-9 and 4-10. This technique can be handy for creating your own signs or names, or for applying dry transfers over rough areas or in tight spaces.

Jim Hediger

Jim Hediger

Fig. 4-11. It's obvious from looking at the paint scheme that Jim Hediger's HO scale Ohio Southern is based on the prototype Detroit, Toledo & Ironton.

Freight-car lettering: What does it all mean?

Pullman-Standard

Jim Hediger

All freight cars carry a variety of lettering. Understanding what it all means can help you create more accurate models. Requirements for prototype cars have changed over the years, but the following list will provide some good guidelines.

1. Road name and herald: This lettering isn't required, and its use varied among railroads and eras. Through the steam era, when the 40-foot boxcar was king, railroads often spelled out their names on one half and included a large herald—or message proudly proclaiming their name passenger trains—on the other half. Car lettering has become more spartan since then, and many modern cars don't include this lettering.

2. Reporting marks: Each owner is assigned a unique set of initials that identify the company or railroad that owns the car. Marks ending in "X" indicate privately owned cars.

3. Number: The car's identifying number. Reporting marks and number are also located on the upper right of each end.

4. Capacity: The car's designed capacity in pounds. Since 1985 Capacity has no longer been required on new cars. The original target date for painting over the Capacity line on older cars was January 1993, but many cars still included this information in 1995.

5. Load Limit: The maximum weight that is allowed for the load itself.

6. Light Weight: The car's weight when empty. If the word "NEW" appears, the weight was taken when the car was built, and the date is stenciled alongside. Cars are periodically reweighed, usually after a repair such as body work or changing wheels or trucks. When this new light weight is stenciled, the initials of the shop performing the work appears to the right, along with the date of the reweighing.

7. Built date: The date the car was built. This information remains the same for the life of the car. On newer cars it appears in the consolidated stencil.

8. Dimensions: The inside and outside measurements of the car. Ice-bunker reefers include bunker capacity in pounds, tank cars include capacity in gallons, and covered hoppers (and some boxcars) include cubic feet.

9. Consolidated stencils: Railroads started to use these panels on freight cars in 1974. Early cars had single panels, then double panels began appearing. The information includes dates and initials of shops that performed work on the car. COTS stands for clean, oil, test, and stencil (brake equipment); RPKD stands for axle repacking; and IDT stands

for in-date (brake) test. Each of these procedures must be performed within specific dates.

10. ACI (Automatic Car Identification) plate: ACI was an optical identification system that used trackside scanners to read colored panels on freight cars (similar to grocery-store scanners). The system was introduced in 1967, and all cars in interchange service were required to have labels by 1970. ACI encountered problems (namely grime), and in 1977 the requirement was eliminated. Railroads generally left the plates on the cars, and many could still be seen on cars in the mid-1990s, albeit in tattered condition.

11. Wheel inspection dot: These marks began appearing in March 1978 when U-1 wheels (made by a certain manufacturer) were found to be defective. All cars of 70-ton or less capacity equipped with 33" wheels had to be inspected. Those found not to have U-1 wheels were painted with a black square and yellow dot; those with U-1 wheels received a white dot. All U-1 wheels had to be replaced by December 1978, and those still in service were restricted. Cars new or repainted in 1979 and later won't have this mark.

12. Plate clearance. This mark signifies that the outside dimensions of this car conform to Plate C (standard) clearance. Railroads use this information to make sure that larger cars (Plate D, etc.) are sent via routes that can handle the dimensions.

Cars often include other lettering, indicating type of wheel, truck, and brake equipment, and car manufacturer. Special features are often highlighted, such as Damage Free (DF) interior load restrainers or cushion underframes of certain cars. Freight cars in dedicated service include information on the materials they carry, as well as information to agents on returning the car to a particular interchange or shipper.

paint, lettering, and striping adds believability, since locomotive builders designed many schemes for railroads, many of which look quite similar.

If you create your own graphics on a computer or by hand, it's possible to transfer black or colored lettering onto plain decal paper using a photocopier or a computer laser printer. The quality won't be as good as that of commercial decals, but it can be a handy technique for one-of-a-kind graphics.

Renumbering factory-painted cars

Sometimes you find just the car or locomotive you need at the hobby shop, already neatly lettered. But what if you need three or four (or more) cars and only one road number is available?

It's often possible to erase the road number (or one or two digits of it) without having to repaint the whole car. You can use a couple of methods, depending upon the type of ink or paint used to letter the model.

Figure 4-13 shows one method to remove lettering using Solvaset and a pencil eraser or cotton swab. If a decal doesn't react to this, try a bit of abrasive cleanser on the tip of a toothpick. The key to both techniques is to work slowly and rub just the lettering, so the underlying paint is not removed.

Some types of lettering are tougher than others, and unfortunately it's not easy to tell which kind your car has until you've started. If the Solvaset or cleanser don't work, use fine sandpaper or a bit of paint remover such as Polly S ELO (Easy Lift-Off). Wash it off the model quickly, because it will soon start to soften the paint under the lettering.

If you do remove some underlying paint, don't panic. Find a model paint that's close to the model's color and touch up the area with a fine-point brush. Once you add decals, the touched-up area won't be noticeable.

If you're only replacing one or two digits of a number, you'll need to find decals that are a very close match to the factory lettering. I like to replace the whole number, so I don't have to be quite as picky.

Apply the decals as you would any others, as in fig. 4-13. Add a coat of flat finish and some weathering and the new numbers will blend right in.

Enhancing factory paint jobs

Figure 4-14 shows some samples of decals that will dress up any models, whether you or Athearn painted them. Consolodated stencils, ACI labels, car-routing chalk marks and scribblings, hazardous-materials placards, wheel inspection dots, and other lettering all help make ordinary models more realistic.

Sources of information

Nothing beats a good photo when you're trying to figure out how to letter a particular locomotive or piece of rolling stock. Magazines and books are great sources for photos. Many new all-color books on specific railroads have been published recently. They are an invaluable resource for modelers looking for lettering information.

Many companies and individuals sell black-and-white photos and color slides of specific equipment—check

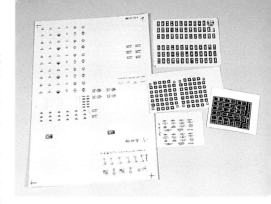

Fig. 4-14. HO decals clockwise from left: hazardous materials placards and scribblings from Microscale; ACI labels from Herald King; and wheel inspection dots, consolidated stencils, and car builder's insignia from Champion.

the display and classified ads in *Model Railroader, Trains,* and other rail-related magazines.

Historical societies are another great source of information. Most societies produce newsletters, magazines, and other publications that contain detailed painting and lettering information that's invaluable if you model a particular railroad.

Most modelers are concerned about getting the right numbers on their locomotives. Magazines that cater to locomotive fans, such as *Diesel Era* and *Extra 2200 South,* often include all-time railroad or model rosters. Books such as *Diesel Locomotive Rosters* (Kalmbach Publishing Co.) list current rosters of North American Railroads.

Railroad Rosters: The Railroad Magazine Series is a book that lists all-time rosters for most North American railroads up to the 1970s.

For information on freight car numbering, the *Official Railway Equipment Register* is tough to beat. This quarterly publication lists all North American freight cars currently in service. Cars are indexed by railroad and private owner, and the listings include capacity and other data. New issues are available from the publisher for around $40. Back issues are often found at swap meets or from dealers in railroadiana—check classified ads in the railroad publications. It's probably sufficient to have one issue from the era you model.

Now that the lettering's in place, let's learn the basics of weathering models!

Fig. 4-12. An ordinary pencil eraser often works well to remove factory lettering; adding a bit of Solvaset can also help.

Fig. 4-13 Add the new decals, then seal them with a clear overcoat.

5 Basics of Weathering
Using drybrushing, washes, and sprays to create a variety of effects

You've just spent numerous hours placing details and airbrushing a great-looking paint job on a locomotive. Why in the world would you want to turn around and gunk it up?

Prototype locomotives and rolling stock begin to show signs of exposure to the elements almost as soon as they leave the paint shop. These effects can range from a light coating of dust to heavy layers of grime and rust.

Structures and other items also show various effects of nature: paint fades and peels, wood turns gray, and painted signs fade.

Adding weathering to your models re-creates these effects, making them more realistic. Weathering also helps to highlight details, making them stand out on your models.

The key to creating realistic weathering effects is to figure out why weathering occurs in real life and then determine the best ways to duplicate it in miniature. To achieve a natural balance, some models should be heavily weathered, some should be quite clean, and most should be somewhere in the middle.

Weathering should follow prototype practices. For example, in the 1950s the Santa Fe kept its passenger trains almost spotless, as fig. 5-1 shows. A model of a Santa Fe passenger car should therefore be quite clean, with perhaps a bit of dust on the trucks.

Southern Pacific freight locomotives are another story. These engines see tough duty on steep mountain grades and in hot deserts. The railroad's many tunnels cause exhaust smoke and grime to build up on locomotives, and this all takes a toll on paint and lettering, as shown in fig. 5-2.

Keep in mind, however, that weathering doesn't have to be heavy to be effective. In fact, it's often the light and subtle highlights that are the most effective on your model.

Fig. 5-1. The sun glistens on the spotless stainless steel passenger cars of Santa Fe's *El Capitan*.

J. David Ingles

Fig. 5-2. Southern Pacific locomotives face tough operating conditions, which wear paint and lettering.

Techniques

I use three basic techniques to do most of my weathering: drybrushing, washes, and oversprays. These methods work well on factory-lettered models, as well as those that you've painted and decaled. In fact, weathering is a great way to hide fuzzy factory lettering.

Fig. 5-3 lists some of my favorite paints for weathering. Flat paints are best for most weathering applications, except for simulating oil and grease. Don't limit yourself to this list. Look at the color of paint, not the name on the bottle, when you're choosing paint for weathering.

Drybrushing

Water-based paints, such as Accu-Flex and Polly S, are good for drybrushing because they can be removed with a damp towel immediately after they are applied. Additionally, there are no annoying and dangerous fumes, common to solvent-based paints.

Begin by dipping a stiff-bristled brush in paint, then wiping off most of the paint on a paper towel, as shown in figs. 5-4 and 5-5. Then, with the almost-dry brush, streak the model. This technique is handy for creating effects of peeling paint, streaked rust stains, grime, and dirt. You can vary the amount of paint on the brush as well as the brush pressure to create different effects. Figure 5-6 shows the finished car.

If you need to control the paint in a narrow area, such as along a rivet line or weld seam, use a guide like the one in figs 5-7 and 5-8 to help. You can also use a similar guide to control weathering sprays.

Drybrushing is hard on brushes, so I generally keep some older ones on hand for this duty—brushes that already have damaged or frayed bristles.

Washes

I use Polly S paints for most washes, thinning 1 part paint with about 6 parts Polly S Airbrush Thinner. You can also thin Polly S with water, but the surface tension of the water sometimes causes the paint to bead on the model surface. Using the alcohol-based

Fig. 5-3. Good weathering colors

Paint	Effect
black, grimy black, weathered black, gray	general grime, dirt
gloss black	oil spills and stains
earth, sand, tan	dust, sand
roof brown, rail brown, various browns	old, dark rust
rust, orange	new, bright rust
white	faded paint, streaked lettering

Fig. 5-4. Dip the tips of the bristles in paint, then wipe off most of the paint on a paper towel.

Fig. 5-5. Streak the brush over the model.

Fig. 5-6. The streaked lettering and rusty rivet lines on this HO Accurail car were all created by drybrushing.

Fig. 5-7. Make a template by cutting slots in a piece of .010" styrene.

Fig. 5-8. This is handy for guiding the brush in narrow areas, such as along the seams of this HO Accurail covered hopper.

Airbrush Thinner helps the paint spread across the surface.

Again, if you don't like the way something turns out, you can wash it off quickly. Another advantage of water-based paint washes is that they won't attack underlying paint the way solvent-based washes can.

Apply washes as shown in figs. 5-9 and 5-10, using a wide brush with soft bristles. Begin the brush stroke at one edge of the surface you are covering and continue it all the way to the other edge without stopping. The result is a streaked look that re-creates the effect of rain washing grime down the side of a car or structure. If you stop or start the stroke in the middle of the surface, you'll leave brush strokes behind.

Washes tend to cling around rivet lines, ribs, ladders, in door cracks, and around other details, just like grime does on prototype equipment. Use black, grimy black, and dark grays to create overall grime effects, or use browns and other rust colors to create rust and corrosion effects.

You can achieve various effects by adding washes in layers. For example, you can use a fine-point brush to apply

Fig. 5-9 (ABOVE). Use a wide brush to apply washes. Fig. 5-10. Notice how washes tend to cling around ribs and other details.

a rust wash over just the rivet lines of a freight car, then follow it with a grimy black wash over the entire car.

When doing this, be sure the underlying wash is thoroughly dry. Otherwise, the second wash can dissolve parts of the underlying wash, leaving a patchy effect. One way is to use a hair dryer on the model for a minute following the first wash. Another way is to seal the first wash by adding a clear overspray.

Oversprays

Light oversprays of paint are great for creating effects such as exhaust soot, smoke residue, dust, and overall grime. Chapter 6 shows several examples of this technique.

Create thin paint mixes for spraying by mixing 1 part paint with about 8 parts thinner. Paints thinned this much are easy to control as you apply them. You can build up effects in layers, with little worry of overdoing an effect in one pass. I've had good results using either Floquil paints with Floquil Airbrush Thinner or Polly S paints thinned with Polly S Airbrush Thinner.

This is one application where an internal-mix airbrush definitely works best. An internal-mix brush atomizes the thin mixes well, turning the paint into a very fine mist—as opposed to an external-mix airbrush, which produces larger, more noticeable droplets.

Sealing weathering

As with decals and dry transfers, it's a good idea to add a clear finish over weathering. Since many weathering

effects are thin mixes or use dry or nearly dry paint, the paint won't stick to the surface as well as a regular coat of paint.

Use a flat, semigloss, or gloss finish, depending upon the overall effect you're trying to create.

Putting it all together

The key to successful weathering is to make it believable. Random splotches and sprays of dust and rust may make a model dirty but probably won't make it realistic.

Take a look at what happens on full-size trains. Photographs are probably the best source of ideas. Keep your camera ready, and take photos of effects you think might are worth modeling. Study photos in books as well.

Keep in mind the era of your railroad. Let's say you model 1970: most model cars with built dates in the late 1960s to 1970 shouldn't be weathered heavily. On the other hand, cars built in the 1950s would be starting to show some heavy wear.

Look at the types of weathering that occurs most often. Rust and dark grime (like exhaust stains) tend to accumulate over time, building up as the months and years go by. Dust, on the other hand, builds up only until the next good rainstorm washes it away.

Once you find a car, locomotive, or general effect you'd like to re-create, determine the best way of duplicating it on a model. There's no right or wrong way to do it, as long as the end result is believable. Now let's put these weathering techniques to use on a few models!

These HO scale Kato SD40s look good straight from the box, but a bit of weathering and a few decals make a big difference in appearance.

6 Weathering Locomotives

Re-creating effects from prototype diesel and steam engines

Locomotives are the focal point of every train. Because of the attention they draw, they deserve some extra attention when it comes to finishing.

Adding a few basic weathering effects and decals will turn any out-of-the-box locomotive into an eye-catcher and will provide an extra touch to engines you paint yourself. Let's start at the bottom and work up.

Trucks and couplers

On many model locomotives, the inner truck frame is made of bright metal; on some other models, this area is made of shiny plastic. Either way, these materials both reflect light and create

unrealistic highlights. Paint these areas flat black, as shown in fig. 6-1, to blend them into the background.

Next, paint the wheel faces a rust color. Brand-new wheels on the prototypes are often a bright orange rust; wheels that have been in service for a while range from dark brown to grimy black. Once the paint dries, then use an eraser or edge of a hobby knife to remove any stray paint from the wheel tread (the part that contacts the rail).

Couplers are also generally some shade of rust. I usually airbrush them with a light coat of paint, as in fig. 6-2. Model paints, especially when airbrushed, are fine enough that they won't interfere with the coupler's moving parts. You can also drybrush

couplers for some variations in color. Be careful when using a brush—don't get any blobs of paint into the spring or hinge.

Grills and fans

Grills on painted diesels, even on newer shells with nice detail, don't have a look of depth. Adding a wash of black paint as shown in fig. 6-3 will make it look as though there's space behind the grill face. The wash tends to settle deep in the grooves, making the grill stand out.

Using a water-based paint makes it easy to correct any mistakes: if you get some paint onto the side of the model, use a damp paper towel to remove it. If

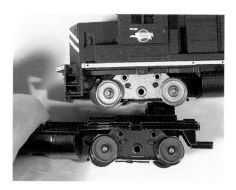

Fig. 6-1. These areas on models are often shiny metal or plastic. Brush-paint them flat black, and paint the wheel sides a rust color before adding the sideframes.

Fig. 6-2. You can safely airbrush Kadee and Micro-Trains couplers to dull the shine of the bright spring and metal parts. This one was done with Polly S Roof Brown, with drybrushed Rust highlights.

Fig. 6-3. Add a black wash to the recessed areas to give grills the appearance of depth.

Mark Watson

Fig. 6-4. Locomotive fan blades appear below the gills. Note also that even though this Norfolk Southern engine is black, exhaust stains are quite apparent.

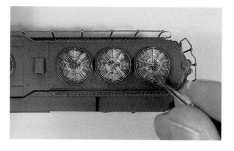

Fig. 6-5. Start by working dull silver or gray paint down onto the molded blades.

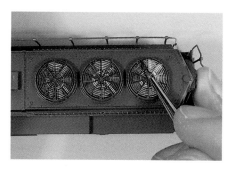

Fig. 6-6. Once the silver dries, use the edge of a brush to paint the grills black.

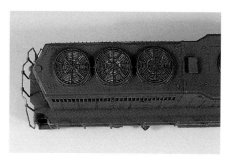

Fig. 6-7. The fans and grills now look like separate pieces.

the paint creeps up onto the grill itself, you can use a pencil eraser to clean it off, or touch it up with a paint that matches the body.

Fan blades on prototype diesels are visible from above, as shown in fig. 6-4. The fans on many plastic diesels in HO and larger scales include molded fan blade detail, but it can be difficult to see. To improve their appearance, start by using a brush to work some Polly S Flat Aluminum into the fan blades as shown in figs. 6-5 and 6-6. For older locomotives use a medium gray. Next, use the edge of a brush to paint black over the grills.

As fig. 6-7 shows, this makes the fan blades and grills appear as separate components. The appearance isn't quite as good as the separate fan and blade details you can add on, but painting is easier, quicker, and less expensive.

Decals

Manufacturers offer many sets of decals that allow you to dress up your locomotives inexpensively. As you can see on the Kato Burlington SD40 and Athearn Rio Grande GP40-2, number boards are among the most prominent improvements you can make to a diesel. ShellScale makes HO scale number board decals in almost every style found on real railroads—fig. 6-8 shows a few of them. Microscale makes similar sets in N, HO, and O scales.

Other important decals include builder's plates, trust plates, door kick-plates, and engine-room door lettering.

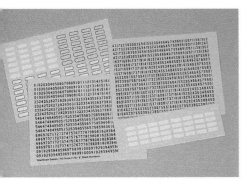

Fig. 6-8. ShellScale makes a tremendous variety of HO number board decals to match specific prototypes, including various styles of numbers, board backgrounds, and gaskets.

Dynamic brakes

Locomotives that operate on steep mountain grades, such as those of Southern Pacific and the former Rio Grande, utilize dynamic braking. Dynamic brakes turn the locomotive's axle-mounted traction motors into generators, creating resistance that slows the train. The electricity generated in this way is dissipated in the form of heat by banks of resistors in a roof-mounted blister.

Dynamic brakes create a tremendous amount of heat. On locomotives that operate in mountainous terrain, the intense heat can bake off the paint around the dynamic brake grids, as shown in fig. 6-9.

To re-create this on the Rio Grande locomotive in fig. 6-10, I airbrushed thinned orange paint vertically down from the grid to simulate primer showing through the black paint.

To create a couple of patches that were down to bare metal and rusting, I used—what else?—real rust. Here's how: Use a knife to scrape some rust off of a piece of metal (I used an old railroad spike). Brush a small patch of Polly S Roof Brown on the model, then sprinkle some of the powdered rust on the paint. The paint will act like glue and hold it in place. Figure 6-11 shows the final results.

This technique takes some time but results in very realistic rust patches that have texture as well as color. You can use this method on freight cars, bridges, or any other detail item.

Overall effects

The photo of the Burlington locomotives shows some other diesel weathering effects. The exhaust soot is an overspray of Polly S Engine Black and Grimy Black, and the dust on the trucks and tank is an overspray of Polly S Earth.

Most locomotives, even those that are fresh from the shop, will have a stain from a fuel spill. Re-create it by

Fig. 6-9. The orange streaks around the dynamic brake blister show how the heat has cooked the paint down to the primer.

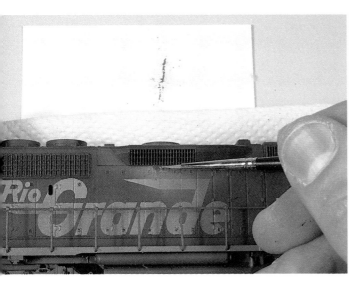

Fig. 6-10. Paint patches of Roof Brown near the blister, then sprinkle on real powdered rust.

Fig. 6-11. The wear around the dynamic brake blister gives the impression that this locomotive has put in some long, hard hours of service.

brushing a patch of gloss or semigloss black paint from the fuel filler down the side of the tank after the other weathering is in place.

Cab units weather differently than hood units. Figure 6-12 shows a prototype F unit that's been out on the road for a while. Notice how the grime begins in a heavy pattern behind the pilot, then rises and feathers out along the side. As fig. 6-13 shows, an overspray of an earth or grime color will capture this look on a model.

Keep an eye out for various paint schemes, and watch for details like rusty cab roofs, white corrosion stains near battery boxes, and peeling lettering. Each scheme will weather differently, depending upon the quality of paint used and the type of service a locomotive sees.

Fig. 6-12. These locomotives often collect grime in a "bow-wave" pattern. Note how the pilot is clean, but the dust starts accumulating behind the pilot and feathers out along the side.

Fig. 6-13. To create the bow-wave effect on a model, airbrush dust or grime colors in a pattern along the lower sides, starting behind the pilot.

Steam locomotives

Contrary to popular belief, steam locomotives aren't all flat black and dull. Look at the Pennsylvania RR K4 in fig. 6-14 and you'll see a shiny finish just visible under various weathering effects.

The weathering of steam locomotives depends largely upon the type of service they're in and how much care the railroads lavish on them. Many railroads kept their front-line passenger engines in pristine condition, scrubbing them down after every run.

Freight locomotives often didn't fare as well, especially during the Depression and other economic hard times, or times of extremely busy service, such as World War II. Like the diesels, steam locomotives that saw tough duty on mountain grades and in tunnels would accumulate grime faster than locomotives in the flatlands.

The smokebox usually starts out silver, graphite, or gray, but weathers to a flat dark gray. The most noticeable weathering effect is from smoke. Soot collects around the smokestack and smokebox, and also along the top of the locomotive and tender. This soot is then washed down the sides of the boiler by water from steam condensation (especially around the steam dome, safety valve, whistle, and bell) and by natural precipitation. Black and dark gray streaks result. White or light gray streaks are sometimes caused by mineral deposits in the boiler water.

Figures 6-15 and 6-16 show how to re-create these effects on a model. Start by drybrushing streaks on top and down the sides of the boiler and by using washes applied with a fine-point brush. Follow this by airbrushing a mix of grimy black and black along the top of the boiler and cab roof, then down the sides over the drybrushing.

Prototype steam locomotive wheels are usually black, and the rods and valve gear can be natural or polished metal, black, or painted other colors. After a while these parts all turn a dirty black color. Builders' photos often show wheels and running boards lined with white paint, but the white was usually painted out before the photographer had his camera put away.

Don Wood

Fig. 6-14. This Pennsy 4-6-2 has streaks of grime down the sides of the smokebox and boiler, but there are still some glossy highlights showing through.

Figs. 6-15 and 6-16. Drybrushing, washes, and oversprays are effective on factory-painted models like this Bachmann Spectrum HO scale K4.

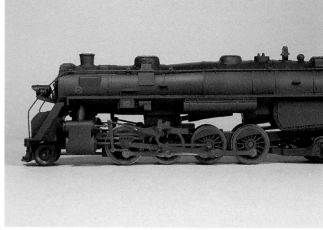

Fig. 6-17. A thinned overspray of black kills the shine on wheels, rods, and valve gear. Build up the effect in thin coats.

Fig. 6-18. Some flat black paint on the exposed part of the motor and drive shaft helps hide these parts.

On many models, such as the HO scale Mantua engine in figs. 6-17 and 6-18, the rods and valve gear are made of shiny metal. To tone them down, set the locomotive on a wired track in a spray booth and run it in a stationary position while airbrushing the wheels, rods, and valve gear with thinned grimy black. By keeping the wheels moving, the weathering will be fairly even. Chapter 11 shows how I did this to a brass locomotive.

A bit of flat black paint does wonders for hiding the motor and drive shaft on many models, as shown on the Mantua locomotive. Don't get paint on the drive shaft at the points where it enters the motor or gearbox.

Most models have a textured black plastic surface to simulate coal. On coal-fired locomotives, like the Bachmann Spectrum K4, I like to add a more realistic coal load. Figures 6-19 and 6-20 show how to do this. Begin by brush-painting flat black across the area (be generous), then pour some scale coal over it and pat it into place. Once it's dry, dump out the excess.

The Bachmann locomotive included an engineer and fireman, which was a nice touch. Unfortunately, they were painted with gloss paint, and the hands and faces were a ghostly white color. I popped them out of the cab and painted them in more realistic colors, then set them back in the cab.

Now that your motive power looks as though it's earning its keep, let's make the rolling stock appear to be working just as hard.

Fig. 6-19 (ABOVE). Spread black paint over the molded plastic coal. Fig. 6-20 (BELOW). Next, sprinkle scale coal over it.

7 Weathering Freight Cars

Methods of distressing factory-painted models as well as those you paint yourself

If you look at a train of freight cars you'll see a tremendous variety of weathering effects, in both the type and the amount of weathering. Most railroads repaint locomotives every few years, and many wash them regularly. However, freight cars sometimes make it through a 20- or 30-year career without visiting a car washer or getting a fresh coat of paint.

Weathering effects vary depending upon the type of service, the region of the country, the car's age, and the type and quality of its finish. This chapter looks at several prototype cars and examine various ways of re-creating those effects.

But first, here are a couple of things you can do to all of your freight cars.

Trucks, wheels, and couplers

Prototype truck sideframes are usually painted black or painted to match the color of the car. However, after a few years of service most take on a grimy black appearance with various rust-colored highlights.

Model trucks, on the other hand, are usually molded in black plastic, which looks exactly like—yes, black plastic. Paint your truck sideframes a base color such as grimy black or roof brown, and then highlight different colors by drybrushing or using washes.

As with locomotives, you'll want to paint wheel faces a rust color. I use Kadee wheelsets on my HO freight cars, so I usually paint several packages of them at once, using various colors from bright rust to grimy black.

You can polish wheel treads on metal wheelsets such as Kadee's using a wire brush in a motor tool after the wheelsets are mounted. This nicely simulates the shiny steel look of prototype wheel treads.

If you really want to go for detailing, here are a couple of neat effects. Wheel faces on the older solid-bearing trucks often became splattered with grease from the journal boxes, as shown in fig. 7-1. You can simulate this by brushing patches of gloss black paint on individual wheel faces.

The roller-bearing adapter on modern roller-bearing trucks is usually a

Fig. 7-1. Wheel faces on solid-bearing trucks, shown here in HO scale, are often shiny black from journal-box grease.

dark red color, as shown in fig. 7-2. Use a fine-point brush to paint it a maroon or boxcar red color, as in fig. 7-3.

Treat the couplers on your freight cars as you did the ones on locomotives—paint them in various tones of rust.

Underframes on model boxcars are usually unpainted plastic, and on other cars the underframe is often painted to match the body. Since prototype underframes bear the brunt of the grime splashed up from the wheels, treat models with sprays and washes of various colors of grime and rust.

Fig. 7-2 (ABOVE). Note the shiny wheel treads and varying rust colors on the wheel faces of these two-year-old Burlington Northern covered hoppers. You can also see the bright rust on the unpainted couplers. Fig. 7-3 (RIGHT). Wheels are usually cleaner on these trucks. Paint the roller-bearing adapters with an oxide red color.

Fig. 7-4. Lettering on prototype cars sometimes peels away, letting rust show through.

Fig. 7-5. To re-create peeling lettering, use a fine-point brush to paint rust colors directly over the lettering. You can make the effect as light or heavy as you need.

Freight car lettering

Lettering on freight cars takes a beating over time. Chapter 5 showed how drybrushing the car color over the lettering makes it look streaked and old. The paint doesn't have to be an exact match—find as close a color as you can.

As in fig. 7-4, parts of the lettering are often missing, with rust showing through. You can simulate this as shown in fig. 7-5, by using a fine brush to paint a dark rust color directly on the lettering. You may have to use a couple of coats to achieve the effect you're looking for.

Sometimes the paint used for lettering chalks over time and then washes down over the car side, as in fig. 7-6. Re-create this as in figs. 7-7 and 7-8 by drybrushing the color of the lettering down the car side below the lettering.

Roofs

Many modelers neglect freight car roofs when weathering. The reason is simple—you don't often see the tops of prototype trains when you're watching them trackside. However, unless you have a very tall layout, chances are you have a bird's-eye view of your models.

Watch a passing train from a bridge and you'll be amazed at the variety of effects on car roofs. In the steam and early diesel eras, boxcars usually had roofs painted the body color, or sometimes black. Many reefers had silver or other light-color roofs to reflect heat.

Most modern boxcars have galvanized steel roofs, which are either their natural dull metallic gray color, as in fig. 7-9, or painted to match the body color. Galvanized roofs on older cars often have large patches of rust, and newer cars have paint overspray from the sides around the edges of the roof.

Figures 7-10 and 7-11 show a couple of ways to treat model roofs. If you weather roofs in assembly-line fashion, it's possible to do a couple of dozen cars in an evening.

Restenciled data

Chapter 4 discussed how freight cars are periodically reweighed, with the new capacity data and weigh date

Fig. 7-6. After 25 years of service without a paint job, the lettering on this **NP** wood chip car is washing down the side. The effect is quite uniform.

Figs. 7-7 and 7-8 (ABOVE AND BELOW). Re-create streaked lettering by drybrushing white below the lettering. Adding oversprays of various weathering colors will help make the effect more uniform.

Fig. 7-9. Boxcar roofs often have paint overspray around the edges, as on the foreground car. The car roof in the background is rusting heavily.

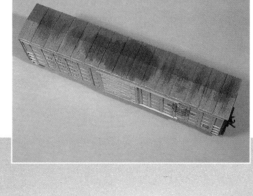

Fig. 7-10. The roof on this Walthers **HO** car started out silver. Paint rust patches with various rust colors, then add a light overspray of grimy black to give the silver a dull, galvanized-steel look.

restenciled on the car. Figure 7-12 shows how this appears, with the old (weathered) data painted over and the new information stenciled in place.

Re-creating this on a model is easy, as in figs. 7-13 and 7-14. Simply add a piece of masking tape over the capacity data before weathering the car. When you peel the tape away, it will look as if the area has been repainted.

Scrapes and dents

Freight cars often get scratched and dented in minor collisions. Figure 7-15 shows a wood chip car with a series of

Fig. 7-11. Lightly dust the edges of a "galvanized" roof with the body color—blue for this **E&C Shops HO** car. Finish with a grimy black overspray. Many boxcar roofs, like this Accurail Frisco boxcar, are painted the body color. Weather them with washes, drybrushing, or oversprays of any dark color.

F. Hol Wagner Jr.

Fig. 7-12. The fresh paint on the restenciled area stands out on this weathered Fort Worth & Denver car.

deep scratches in its side. These areas have begun to rust.

One way to model this is by scratching the model with a scriber, then coloring the scratch. Figures 7-16 and 7-17 show how to do this by sliding a ball of paper towel dampened with a black paint wash over the side of the car. This technique has the added benefit of creating streaks in the lettering. The photo also shows how to simulate faded paint by using a thinned overspray of white.

Figs. 7-13 (TOP RIGHT) and 7-14 (ABOVE). Adding a piece of masking tape over the data before weathering this HO Accurail car re-created the effect of restenciling.

Fig. 7-15. After 20-plus years, a car is entitled to have some scars and scrapes. Notice how the ribs have lost much of their paint.

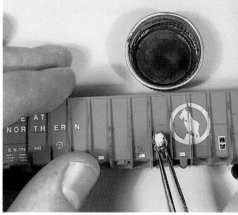

Fig. 7-16. To create rusty gouges, start by carving scratches. I used a scriber on this car. Using a balled-up piece of paper towel wet with a black paint wash, smear it down the side. This deposits paint in the scratches.

Fig. 7-17. Finish the car with an overspray of thinned white to fade the paint, and some drybrushed rust.

Figure 7-18 shows a car that looks as though it's been sideswiped. The rest of the car looks almost new, but the gouges, along with several scrapes on the lettering, have begun to rust.

You can model this as shown in fig. 7-19. You could also add patches of real rust, as shown in Chapter 6.

Flatcar decks

Most model flatcars use molded plastic to simulate wood. One way to make them look more realistic is to replace the plastic deck with one made of stripwood. Figure 7-20 shows another way, using paint to make the plastic more realistic.

Start by roughing up the deck with coarse sandpaper. Paint the deck grimy black, then follow that with drybrushing and washes of black and various grays and browns. Seal each layer of weathering with a light coat of Testor's Dullcote. Finish with a light airbrush dusting of grimy black.

Caboose windows

In the early 1980s the Federal Railroad Administration began requiring railroads to use shatter-proof safety glass for all windows in locomotives and cabooses. Since this glass is very expensive, many railroads chose to cover windows in cabooses instead of replacing them. In many cases, like the Soo Line caboose in fig. 7-21, the railroad didn't repaint the entire car—just the plates over the windows.

Figure 7-22 shows how to model this effect using a prepainted kit. Begin by weathering the car. Paint .010"

Fig. 7-18. New cars can also have rust. This BN car had a close encounter with something that left gouges, which have begun to rust.

Fig. 7-19. I gouged this HO Accurail car in the same way as the N scale wood chip car, then painted on additional patches of rust.

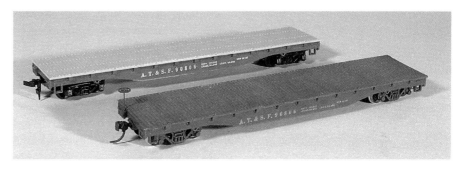

Fig. 7-20. These old HO Tyco train set cars have plastic decks, but the decks include some nice wood-grain details. I painted them by drybrushing and adding washes of gray, grimy black, and black in several layers. I also added new trucks, a brake wheel, and body-mounted Kadee couplers.

styrene to match the caboose, then cut it to fit snugly in the window openings. Apply plastic cement sparingly from the inside to hold the styrene in place.

Add some more light weathering, and your caboose is complete.

Auto racks

Most model auto carriers have roofs and side panels molded in either silver plastic or painted silver. Start by giving these parts a light airbrush coat of

thinned grimy black to tone down the silver and make it look more like galvanized steel.

The prototype Union Pacific car in fig. 7-23 has a large rusted area on its roof. Natural precipitation has washed rust stains down the sides of the car. Figures 7-24 and 7-25 show how to model this.

Start by painting rust patterns on the roof with Polly S Roof Brown and Rust. Add highlights, using various oranges and other rust colors. Airbrush

Fig. 7-21. It's obvious where the windows once were on this Soo Line caboose.

Fig. 7-22. Begin by giving the car an initial coat of weathering. Cut styrene to fit in the window openings, paint it the original car color (it doesn't have to be an exact match), and glue it in place. Finish with some light weathering.

Fig. 7-23. Stains from the rusted roof on this Union Pacific auto rack have washed down the sides.

Figs. 7-24 (LEFT) and 7-25 (BELOW). Painting the side panels and roof of this Walthers HO car prior to assembly made it easier to control the effects.

then add dry transfer numbers over it.

The insides of gondolas are just as important as the outsides. Use a wide, flat brush to paint the floor and inner walls with a mix of flat black and rail brown. Use the brush to mix and blend the colors, streaking them vertically up the sides. While the paint is still wet, sprinkle on some real rust. (I scraped mine from an old railroad spike.)

Finish the car with oversprays of thinned grimy black and earth.

Modeling specific loads

Oftentimes, the weathering on prototype freight cars is influenced by the loads they carry. With some paint and a bit of time you can re-create these cars. They can help identify industries, indicate the priority of a train, and give your railroad a reason for operation.

Cement-covered hoppers

Powdered cement and limestone (used to make cement) are dense, heavy materials that are usually shipped in short two-bay covered hoppers. As fig. 7-28 shows, any spilled material on the roof is carried down the sides by rain, leaving white streaks on the car sides. These materials are very fine powders, which often dust over the entire car.

rust colors on the side panels before installing them. Add drybrushed streaks on the panels and car, then glue the panels in place.

Finish the car by airbrushing thinned grimy black and earth on the underframe, sides, and ends.

Gondolas

Because they often have loads dropped into them at steel mills, scrap yards, and other industries, gondolas are usually the most damaged cars on a railroad. Figure 7-26 shows a former Railgon car that's seen better days.

An HO Model Die Casting car lettered for Railgon was a great starting point, as fig. 7-27 shows. Use a pencil eraser to remove the reporting marks and a lot of the lettering.

The scribblings near the car number came from a Microscale decal set, but you can create customized scribblings with a white artist's pencil. You can also use white typewriter correction ribbon by positioning the ribbon over the car, then writing on the reverse side so that the white scribbling is left on the car.

Paint rust patches where the lettering had been, and also along a few other areas on the sides and ends. Paint over part of the capacity data with boxcar red paint, as on the prototype,

Fig. 7-26. This old Railgon car has new reporting marks courtesy of the Baltimore & Ohio. Gons are probably the most damaged cars on railroads.

Fig. 7-27. Since they're open cars, the insides of gondolas are as important as the exteriors. Real rust, secured by paint, adds some nice texture.

Fig. 7-28. Telltale signs of a limestone or cement-service car are the white streaks down the sides.

Fig. 7-29. A few drybrushed streaks and an overspray of white create a distinctive car.

Fig. 7-30. Tank cars in fuel and oil service take on a grungy black appearance. This former Chicago Great Western car still sports its CGW logo 25 years after the road was merged into the Chicago & North Western.

Fig. 7-31. To re-create the effects of the prototype CGW car on this N scale Micro-Trains car, add a masking tape patch before weathering with grimy black and black weathering sprays.

Fig. 7-32. Black and grimy black weathering sprays can be very effective on black cars. The grimy black tones down the stark color of the car, and both work to fade the lettering.

Linn H. Westcott

Fig. 7-33. These cars are often covered with telltale greenish-yellow splashes of dried sulfur.

Fig. 7-34. Begin by airbrushing and drybrushing a yellow mix around the dome and down the sides. Add black streaks over the yellow.

As in fig. 7-29, you can re-create this effect on a model by drybrushing white around the roof hatches and down the sides of a car. Add a light overspray of thinned white paint to make it look as if the car has a coating of fine powder.

Oil tank cars

Any tank car in petroleum service will be identifiable after a few years on the road. Figure 7-30 shows a company-service fuel car. You can see that it started out life painted maroon but now has an overall grungy black appearance—one reason why most tank cars in such service are black.

Creating a model is fairly simple. Figures 7-31 and 7-32 show how oversprays of thinned black and grimy black re-create the overall oily appearance of these cars. Streaks of semigloss or gloss black around the tank dome simulate minor spills.

Even on a black car, black oversprays are effective, especially in the way they fade the lettering, as on the UTLX car.

Sulfur tank cars

These cars, which carry molten sulfur, are quite distinctive. As they're loaded, the yellow-green liquid spills and splatters around the dome, top, and sides of

the car. As it dries, it flakes off in patches and streaks, leaving the cars looking like the one in fig. 7-33.

To model this, as shown in fig. 7-34, start with bright yellow paint and add green until the color starts to appear more green than yellow. Airbrush this mix heavily around the dome. (This is one time when you want the paint to splatter a bit.) Drybrush some additional paint down the sides. When that dries, use a brush to streak black over some areas of the yellow to simulate the patches of sulfur that have peeled away.

Tank cars in dedicated service are generally stenciled with their commodities. "MOLTEN SULPHUR"

Fig. 7-35. Phosphoric acid has left white streaks down the sides of this car.

Fig. 7-36. To replicate the effects on the prototype phosphoric acid car, drybrush streaks of white down the sides. Add commodity stenciling like that on the sulfur car.

stenciled on the sides adds a nice touch to these cars. I did it with Gothic dry-transfer lettering from Clover House. The lettering is quite small, but applying the individual letters isn't as tough as it looks and the results are worth the effort.

In regard to spelling—"sulphur" is the most common spelling for the car stenciling, but "sulfur" appears on some cars. I've even seen some cars that had "sulfur" in a company logo but "sulphur" on the product stenciling!

Chemical tank cars

Tank cars are used to carry a wide variety of chemicals. Like the sulfur cars, these cars generally have their contents stenciled on their sides, making them easy to identify.

Different chemicals create various effects when they're spilled on cars. For example, the phosphoric acid car in fig. 7-35 has light-colored streaks down its sides because of spills. To model it, stencil the sides in the same manner as you stenciled the sulfur car. Then drybrush white down the sides as shown in fig. 7-36.

You can do the same with other chemical cars. Keep your eyes open and your camera handy.

Piggyback trailers and containers

If you model today's railroading, you may have more trailers and containers on your layout than boxcars.

Let's start with trailer wheels. The hubs are often white, although some are black and some are painted to match the trailer color. In any case, use a fine-point brush to give them a base coat of silver. Testor's Silver covers well in one coat when applied with a brush, and provides a good base for other colors. When it dries, paint the hubs the final color, as in fig. 37.

You can also use a brush to dab a bit of red paint on the rear lights and orange on the running lights on the front and sides of trailers. Microscale decal sets 87-852 (HO scale), 60-852 (N), and 48-406 (O) include decals for lights, trailer manufacturer markings, mud flaps, and other data. Chapter 8 shows some of these.

The front corners of trailers and containers receive a coating of soot from truck exhausts. Simulate this as shown in fig. 7-37, by airbrushing a light coat of thinned black on the upper front corners.

Where trailers and containers have sustained heavy damage, such as from the shifting of a load, repairs might include a new side panel. Create this effect by masking off a side panel, weathering the trailer, then removing the tape as shown in fig. 7-37. This technique can also be used to show a door that's been replaced.

As fig. 7-38 shows, containers get pretty banged up from being picked up and loaded onto ships, trains, and chassis. Figure 7-39 shows how to re-create this on models.

Now that we've looked at painting, decaling, and weathering, let's put it all together and try a few projects from start to finish.

Fig. 7-37. Some soot, a repaired side panel, running lights, and painted wheel hubs improve the realism of trailers.

Fig. 7-38. Notice the dark streaks on the blue container near the latch bars. This distinctive weathering, found on many containers and trailers, is caused by grime kicked up by rail wheels on "spine" container cars.

Fig. 7-39. To create patched areas as on these N scale Walthers models, place small pieces of masking tape on them, then add weathering. Since well container cars ride so low to the ground, they pick up a lot of grime. Re-create it with oversprays of black and grimy black.

8 A Trio of Basic Painting Projects

Tackling two freight cars and a piggyback
trailer from start to finish

A Milwaukee Road cov-
ered hopper, built in
1973, is showing its age
in this June 1994 photo.

Milwaukee Road covered hopper

Once you've done a couple of basic painting and decaling projects as shown in Chapter 4, you're ready for a project like this one. This Milwaukee Road grain car is a good second or third painting project. The paint scheme is fairly simple, with one color, and the side panels make the car distinctive.

The prototype Milwaukee Road bought and leased several hundred of these Pullman-Standard cars in the early 1970s to handle grain. Many still wear their (now much worn) original paint into the mid-1990s, as the color prototype photo shows.

Modeling

Start by assembling the model. The HO scale InterMountain kit I used is

beautifully detailed but takes a few hours to put together. The InterMountain car has 18 side ribs, as does prototype car no. 100974, but you can also use Athearn's 16-rib car.

If you plan to keep the car looking fairly new, you can glue the roof hatches in place. My intention was to model a car that had been in service for a while and had lost its original hatches, so I left the roof hatches off but placed masking tape over the edges of the opening.

Don't add the couplers or coupler covers yet. Instead, place strips of masking tape over these areas to keep paint out.

Make the side lettering panels from .015" styrene. Cut them long enough to reach the outside of the appropriate side ribs. They should be tall enough to

just clear the lettering in the Champion decal set. Glue them in place.

Painting

It can be tough to paint closed cars such as this one because there's no way to stick a painting handle into the shell. I use a simple jig, shown in fig. 8-1, made from round toothpicks inserted into squares of ceiling tile. The toothpicks go into the holes for the truck-mounting screws to hold the model upright.

The Milwaukee Road painted these cars Federal Yellow, a yellow-orange color. Use a Floquil mix of 3 parts Reefer Yellow and 2 parts Reefer Orange. Then mixed 3 parts of this mix to 1 part Floquil Airbrush Thinner for spraying.

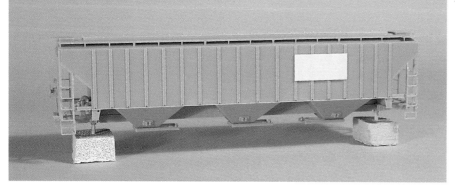

Fig. 8-1. Toothpicks stuck in ceiling tile hold the car upright for painting.

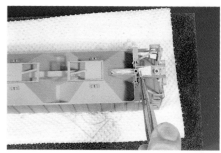

Fig. 8-2. Masking this area makes it easier to add the couplers later.

Fig. 8-3. Carefully align the letters as you add them.

Fig. 8-4. Once each decal is in place, add Champion Decal Set using a soft brush.

Fig. 8-5. Slice any air bubbles with a sharp knife, then add more setting solution.

Fig. 8-6. Here's what the car looks like without weathering.

Airbrush the entire car with the mix. The yellow won't cover right away, so apply several thin coats. Be sure to spray from different angles inside the ends and around the running boards and hatches. Airbrush the corrugated roof hatches separately.

Let the Floquil dry for a day. To help the flat paint accept decals better, give the sides and upper ends two light coats of Floquil Crystal Cote. Remove the masking tape from the roof and coupler pockets, as in fig. 8-2.

While that's drying, use a brush to paint the trucks with a mix of Polly S Roof Brown and Grimy Black. Paint the wheel faces a rust color—I used Polly S Roof Brown mixed with Rust.

Decals

Add the decals using the techniques described in Chapter 4. Start with the large "MILWAUKEE," applying the letters individually, as in fig. 8-3. Cut each letter as close to the printing as possible, then soak the decal in water for a minute.

Slide the decal into place on the body, remembering to keep the decal wet while positioning it with a brush or tweezers. Once it's in position, use the

Fig. 8-7. Use a wide brush to add the wash to the sides.

Fig. 8-8. A pencil eraser will take some of the weathering off the car ribs.

corner of a paper towel to soak up any excess water. Use a brush to add setting solution around the edges as shown in fig. 8-4.

Any time you have a long string of individual letters, it's important to keep the letters aligned horizontally. I find I can do this successfully by sighting down the side of the car as I add each letter. On ribbed-side cars such as this one, you can also carefully lay a straightedge down to check alignment. On this car, the top of the letters should align with the top of the "resourceful" side panel.

Continue adding the rest of the decals, including consolidated stencils (the black boxes with white trim) from a Champion set and an ACI plate (the striped rectangle) from a Herald King set.

Once the decals are dry, check them for trapped air bubbles. These appear as shiny areas, as in fig. 8-5. Use a sharp hobby knife to carefully cut through these areas (cut through the decal without marking the paint), then reapply setting solution. Use a wet paintbrush to wipe away any smears of decal glue or setting solution.

When the area around the "W" dried on my model, there was a thin strip along the rib where the decal pulled away and left the body color showing through. This was easy to touch up using a fine-tip brush and a bit of flat black paint.

Seal the decals with a clear finish. I gave the model a light coat of Testor's Dullcote mixed 1:1 with lacquer thinner. Airbrush the couplers with a thinned mix of Floquil Rail Brown, then add the trucks and couplers.

If you want a model of a new car, stop now—fig. 8-6 shows the finished car in nearly mint condition.

Weathering

The color photo of the prototype car shows what these cars looked like after almost 20 years of service. If you want to weather your model, you don't have to take it to that degree—just stop wherever you like.

Start with the roof hatches. On covered hoppers, these frequently get swapped between cars, and they're often replaced because of damage. Look carefully at the color prototype photo and you'll see two different types of covers (and only one yellow one).

Since the InterMountain kit includes two styles of hatches, I airbrushed the plain covers Accu-Flex Reefer White. I mounted one yellow and three white hatches on the car, then glued them in place.

A black wash does a nice job of re-creating the overall grimy cast of the prototype car. Use a mix of 1 part Polly S Engine Black and 6 parts Polly S Airbrush Thinner and apply it as shown in fig. 8-7. Start with the sides and roof,

then finish with a coat on the underframe, hopper bays, and ends.

I added an overspray of the thinned black. Load up the airbrush with the black mix and spray it over the entire car until you get the effect you're looking for. With the airbrush it's handier to get paint inside the intricate ends than with a brush and a wash.

Notice that the ribs on the prototype car are lighter than the car sides. As shown in fig. 8-8, you can produce this effect by rubbing the ribs lightly with a pencil eraser. This helps bring out a lighter color.

Whether you were aiming for a new or well-used appearance, you now have a distinctive model that you can't buy off the shelf.

BILL OF MATERIALS: GRAIN CAR

Champion decals
HC-671 Milwaukee Road covered hopper
Decal Set
HD-32 consolidated stencil decals, Western U.S.

Floquil
110004 Crystal Cote
110030 Reefer Orange
110031 Reefer Yellow

Herald King decal
ACI labels

InterMountain
PS-2CD covered hopper kit

Kadee
5 couplers
520 33" wheelsets

Polly S
410010 Engine Black
410013 Grimy Black
410070 Roof Brown
410073 Rust

Testor Corp.
1160 Dullcote

Miscellaneous
.015" styrene

Pacemaker boxcar

Although it is attractive and colorful, this New York Central Pacemaker boxcar is a relatively simple two-color paint scheme. A multicolor freight car like this one is a good warm-up to painting a multicolor locomotive.

These cars first appeared in 1946 when the NYC introduced its Pacemaker fast freight service, designed to speed handling times on intraline LCL (less-than-carload) shipments.

The NYC selected a group of 1,000 home-built boxcars for this service, nos. 174000–174999, and painted them in a distinctive vermilion-and-red scheme. In the photo of the prototype, you'll notice that the lettering on these cars is greatly simplified compared to that on a standard boxcar. Since these cars were used only on the NYC, they didn't carry standard dimensional data and other information required for interchange.

This HO scale model reflects one of these cars as they appeared when originally painted. Cars painted after 1949 wore black lettering on the lower half of the body. In 1954 the NYC received an additional 25 Pacemaker boxcars, Pullman-Standard PS-1 cars numbered 175000–175024. They featured 8-foot, six-panel Superior doors and complete dimensional data.

NYC 174235

The Accurail 40-foot steel boxcar differs slightly from the prototype Pacemaker boxcars, in that the Pacemaker cars had a 10'-0" inside height, 6" shorter than the model (and most other new cars of that period). The ends, roof, and trucks also differ slightly, but the model is close enough for the purpose. The model has 6-foot Youngstown doors, which match prototype car nos. 174000–174249 (the remainder had 6-foot Superior seven-panel doors).

Start by giving the boxcar shell and floor/underframe a good scrubbing in warm water and dish detergent, then let the parts air dry.

Spray the entire car with a Scalecoat mix of 2 parts White and 1 part Erie Lackawanna Gray. Thin this mix 1:1 with Scalecoat Thinner for spraying and use about 18 pounds of pressure.

Apply a light first coat, but be sure the paint goes on wet. The light coat will ensure that the paint's solvent doesn't craze the plastic surface. The following coats can be heavier. Allow the paint to dry for at least 48 hours in a dust-free area.

While you're waiting for the shell to dry, add the brake gear to the underframe and paint it black. I used a 1:1 mix of Accu-Flex Flat Black and Grimy Black. I used the same mix on the trucks. I also substituted Kadee 33" wheelsets, painting the wheel sides Polly S Roof Brown and polishing the wheel treads with a wire brush in a motor tool.

Mask the area that's to remain gray as shown in fig. 8-9. Use thin strips of masking tape to outline the area, then use wider strips combined with pieces of paper. I try to use paper whenever possible—the less masking tape that's on the body, the lower the risk of removing underlying paint.

As with many multicolor schemes, masking is the most time-consuming part of the project. Take your time, and make sure that the tape edge is burnished tightly to the body. For this I use a flat toothpick with the end cut to a chisel point.

Adding the red

Mix Scalecoat Pacemaker Red 1:1 with thinner and spray the unmasked portion of the car. Apply a light initial coat along the mask lines, and aim the airbrush away from the masking tape edge. When this light first coat dries it will help seal the edge of the tape. Add additional coats of red until the car is covered.

Let the car dry 20 minutes or so before removing the mask. Hold the car from the inside, and don't touch the red paint. Peel away the mask, bending the tape back sharply against itself as shown in fig. 8-10.

If you're having problems lifting a piece of tape from the shell, don't use tweezers or other sharp metal objects to lift it. Instead, cut a small piece of wood to a chisel point and slide it carefully under a corner. When you've got a corner lifted, use tweezers to remove the tape.

If the masking tape has lifted any gray paint, use a brush to carefully touch up these areas. I had to touch up small areas along the paint seam on each end. When masking the car I hadn't noticed that the red should continue under the doors, so I touched up these areas with a brush. Set the car aside to dry for 48 hours.

The ladders and grab irons on these

cars were painted black. This can be a challenge to re-create on cars like this where the details are molded in place, but if you take a bit of care the job isn't that tough.

Figure 8-11 shows how to paint the ladders. Use the side of a brush to paint only the flat front surfaces of the ladders with Accu-Flex Flat Black. By trying to paint the sides you run the risk of getting black paint on the body side, which would be very noticeable and distracting.

By painting only the front surface, the body colors on the side of the ladder blend into the background, and the black front surface seems to stand away from the body instead of being molded in place.

Use the same technique to paint the grabs on the left of each side. On these features, you'll have to use the brush point to carefully touch the flat anchors of the grabs.

Decals and clear coat

Scalecoat's high-gloss finish makes applying the decals a breeze. Trim the Champion lettering as close to the images as possible. Once each is in place, use a brush to add Champion's Decal Set around the edges. It doesn't take much setting solution on gloss surfaces. Let the decals dry, then poke any air bubbles with a knife point and apply more setting solution.

Because I wanted this car to appear almost new, I limited the weathering to a light overspray of Grimy Black on the roof, ends, and sides. To seal the decals and weathering and tone down the gloss surface, I airbrushed the car with a light coat of

Testor's Dullcote, mixed 1:1 with lacquer thinner.

Add the trucks and couplers to the underframe and then top it off with the shell, and your boxcar is ready to haul parcels along the New York Central.

Fig. 8-9. Start masking with thin strips along the paint line, then add wider pieces of tape with paper to cover the rest of the car.

Fig. 8-10. Pull the tape back sharply across itself as you pull it off.

Fig. 8-11. Use the side of a brush to touch the front surfaces of the ladders and grab irons with black paint.

Piggyback trailers are frequently damaged in service, but this makes them distinctive and worth modeling.

Preferred 45 piggyback trailer

If you model contemporary railroads, trailers and containers could make up a majority of the traffic. So in many ways the piggyback trailer of today is like the 40-foot boxcar of 1940—worthy of as much detail and attention as any freight car.

Although this HO scale trailer has some distinctive details, it isn't a difficult project. At first glance it looks like a one-color (white) trailer, but the aluminum trim and roof make it a two-color project. Athearn's 45-foot trailer is a good starting point.

Body repairs

As the prototype photo shows, some of the lettering has disappeared as a result of repairs. New panels were added to the right side and front. This made the trailer distinctive.

Figures 8-12 and 8-13 show how I added the simulated replacement side panel. Scribe a horizontal line to match the top of the "f" and "d" from the lettering. I also used a scriber to add new rivets along the seam, although this probably wasn't necessary.

Add a small piece of styrene next to the taillights to hold the license plate.

Painting

Airbrush the sides, front, and rear of the body with Accu-Flex Reefer White. This sprays well at approximately 33 pounds of pressure. While that dries, add the landing gear and wheel bogies

to the floor (don't add the wheels yet). Airbrush the underbody assembly with a 1:1 mix of Accu-Flex Engine Black and Grimy Black.

Brush-paint the wheel hubs white. Be careful not to get any paint on the

tires, but don't be overly concerned with getting the paint on evenly—we'll fix that later with some weathering. Assemble the wheels and add them to the underframe, along with a pair of .005" styrene mud flaps, as shown in

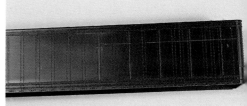

Figs. 8-12 and 8-13. Use a scriber to create the appearance of replaced side panels.

Fig. 8-14. Use cyanoacrylate adhesive (CA) to glue a piece of .020" brass wire across the rear of the bogies. Add the .005" styrene mud flaps to the wire with more CA.

Fig. 8-15. Trim the "Preferred 45" decal to match the repair line scribed on the side.

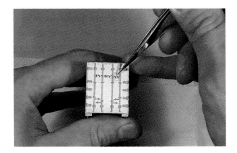

Fig. 8-16. Cut the decals to fit between the latch bars.

fig. 8-14. Paint these Engine Black.

Moving back to the body, use strips of masking tape to cover the sides and front in preparation for airbrushing the roof and trim silver. I used a mix of 3 parts Polly S Flat Aluminum and 2 parts Polly S Airbrush Thinner and airbrushed it at approximately 25 pounds of pressure. Remove the masking as soon as the paint dries.

Use a fine-point brush to paint the hinges, latches, and related hardware on the rear doors with aluminum.

Decals

Start on the right side of the trailer with the simulated replacement side panel. Cut out the large "Preferred 45" decal, trimming off the top of it as shown in fig. 8-15. Apply the decal so that the trimmed edge matches the "repair" line on the trailer. Use Micro Sol to get the decals to settle down around the rivets and seams.

Now add the Milwaukee Road herald and reporting marks. Although the prototype car has had its herald painted over and new reporting marks added, I decided to keep the markings intact. Microscale set no. 87-852 includes decals for the running lights. Do the same on the front of the trailer, trimming the rear of the Preferred logo to match the seam.

Figure 8-16 shows how I added the decals to the rear doors. Trim them into pieces that fit between the latch bars. Cut thin strips out where the lettering would pass under the latch bars. Add the mud flap decals, "wide turn" warning decal, and license plate as shown in fig. 8-17.

Poke any decal bubbles with a sharp knife and reapply Micro Sol. Repeat this until all of the decals are snugly on the body.

Details and weathering

Slide the body into place on the floor assembly. Use a touch of plastic cement in the seam to make sure that everything's secure.

Start the weathering by drybrushing some dark rust colors around the landing gear and the wheel bogies.

Cut a piece of masking tape to fit on the side over the "replacement panel" as shown in fig. 8-18. This will keep that area clean for the first layer of weathering. Mix a batch of 1 part Polly S Black, 1 Part Grimy Black, and 10 parts Polly S Airbrush Thinner. Spray

this mix lightly on the body, underframe, and wheels. Use a hair dryer to dry it for a minute, then remove the masking tape.

Add another light coat of weathering, including a bit of airbrushed "exhaust soot" on the upper front corner. Once the weathering is complete, give the model a light coat of Dullcote to seal everything.

Your trailer is ready to ride the next "pig" train out of town.

Fig. 8-17 (LEFT). The license plate, mud-flap decals, and running lights add a nice touch to the rear and sides.

Fig. 8-18 (ABOVE). Add a piece of masking tape to the repaired area before weathering the trailer.

RIGHT: Chicago Great Western F3A no. 108-A was six years old when this photo was taken at the railroad's Oelwein, Iowa, hub in 1954.

Collection of J. David Ingles

9 Chicago Great Western F3 A and B

A multicolor scheme with lots of curved striping

As the Electro-Motive Division began producing large numbers of F units in the 1940s, EMD's styling department created many beautiful paint schemes that highlighted the F units' distinctive lines.

The same factor that made these schemes so attractive (and popular among today's modelers), caused them to fade from favor on prototype railroads. Their complex multicolor paint schemes with lots of striping were too time-consuming to apply. By the late 1950s railroads were replacing these schemes with simpler one-color schemes, or two-color schemes with less striping.

Among these early flashy schemes, the Chicago Great Western's maroon and red was among the most attractive.

The railroad became known for running long, heavy trains using matched sets (A units at each end with B units between) of up to six or seven F units. Fig. 9-1 shows the numbers worn by these locomotives.

I decided to model an A-B set of F3s using a pair of HO scale Stewart models. The CGW bought their F3s in two different periods. The orders from each period, known as phases, have different body features. Number 108-A is a late Phase II F3, characterized by low radiator fans and screen wire covering the side panels between its portholes. Number 101-B is an early F3B, as indicated by the high shrouded roof fans.

The paint scheme, with its striping and intricate curves, looks difficult, but if you follow the procedures step by

step it isn't overwhelming. You can use the same techniques for re-creating other paint schemes.

Body details

The Stewart models are beautifully detailed, but as with most injection-molded styrene shells, a few areas need cleaning up. Start by removing the shells from the frames and the clear plastic "glass" from the shells.

On the A unit, remove the mold parting lines on the nose and cab roof with a hobby knife and fine sandpaper. When you're sanding models, start with 220-grit and work your way up to 600-grit. It pays to take your time with this, because any flaws in the shell will show through the paint.

Fig. 9-1. Chicago Great Western F units

Nos.	Model	Year built
101–106A	F3A	1947
101–106B	F3B	1947
101–104D	F3B	1949
105–106D	F7B	1949
107A–112A	F3A	1948
107–112B	F3B	1948
107–112D	F7B	1949, 1950
113–115A	F3A	1949
113–115D	F7B	1950
116A, C	FP7 *	1950
116B, D, E, F, G	F7B	1950, 1951
150–152	F3A*	1948, 1949
153–156	F7A*	1949

* Equipped with steam generator for passenger service
All units except 150–156 equipped with dynamic brakes

Fig. 9-2. Fill any scratches or gaps with body putty, then sand the area smooth with fine sandpaper.

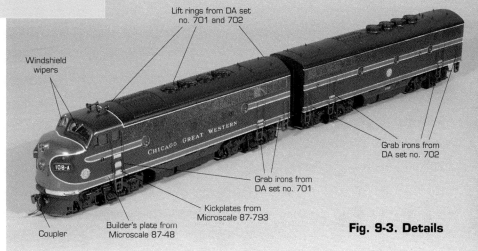

Fig. 9-3. Details

- Lift rings from DA set no. 701 and 702
- Windshield wipers
- Grab irons from DA set no. 702
- Grab irons from DA set no. 701
- Kickplates from Microscale 87-793
- Builder's plate from Microscale 87-48
- Coupler

Sometimes it's necessary to fill small gaps with body putty as shown in fig. 9-2. Use a toothpick to add putty (I used Dr. Microtools red putty), let it dry, then sand the area smooth. The photo shows an X-Acto sanding stick, a handy tool for sanding in tight areas.

Figure 9-3 shows the additional details you can add to the engines. Drill no. 80 holes for all of the lift rings and grab irons. Use cyanoacrylate adhesive (CA) to glue the lift rings in place from inside the shell, but don't add the grab irons yet—they'll be added once the paint and decals are in place.

Prepare the shells for painting by scrubbing them with a toothbrush and dish detergent in warm water. Rinse them thoroughly and allow them to dry.

Painting

I used Accu-Flex paints: EL Maroon and Caboose Red. Start by painting both shells red. Dial the air pressure to approximately 35 pounds and apply the paint in even coats, as described in Chapter 3. Just a couple of coats should cover the light gray plastic.

Look at the models under a bright light to make sure that you've got all of the nooks and crannies coated. To speed the drying time, go over each

shell with a hair dryer for no more than a minute. With Accu-Flex, it's safe to apply masking tape after the paint dries for 20 minutes.

Masking

The toughest and most tedious part of most schemes like this one is masking for the second color. To ensure that the decal stripes fit properly, it's critical that the separation lines are in the right locations. It's also important that all curved lines, such as the nose curves on the A unit, match from side to side. If they are off by even a few scale inches the model will look off-balance and the effect will be lost.

Any diagrams or photos you can find will help you mask the model

properly. Microscale includes a good painting diagram with this decal set, and I had the prototype photo shown in this chapter to guide me.

Begin by cutting masking tape for the nose curves. To be sure the tape matches the decals, cut the tape using the decal stripes as a pattern, as shown in fig. 9-4. Apply the curved masks to the model as shown in fig. 9-5. Check reference points such as grab irons, number boards, headlights, and sand filler hatches against diagrams and prototype photos to help you place the masks. Use the same techniques to cut and apply the middle side stripes.

Once the curved masks are on the model and you're satisfied with the placement, use additional pieces of tape to mask the remaining areas. Note that

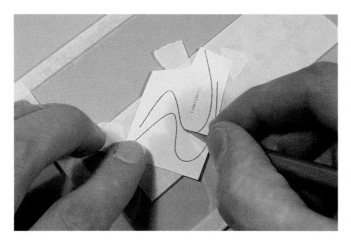

Fig. 9-4. Place a length of masking tape on a piece of glass. Using a photocopy of the decal stripes, cut the curved pattern onto the masking tape.

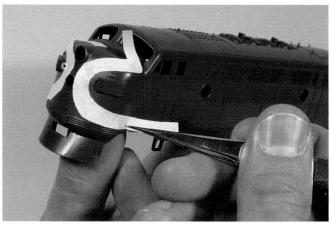

Fig. 9-5. Use reference points such as the number boards and classification lights when applying the compound-curve masks.

Fig. 9-6. Fill the remaining area around the nose with additional tape, then burnish all of the tape edges before spraying the maroon.

both side stripes wrap about six inches around the ends.

Burnish the tape edges with the back side of your fingernail without scratching the red paint. Be sure the tape is snug around rivet strips and other details.

Second color

Figure 9-6 shows the A unit ready for painting. Airbrush the models with maroon, without spraying directly toward a tape edge. Make sure you've coated all of the exposed areas, dry the shells with a hair dryer, set the models aside, and take a deep breath.

The roofs on these engines are black. The masking for this is simpler than for the sides. Use the photocopy-pattern technique for cutting the curved mask at the front of the A-unit roof, then use wide masking tape to cover the bodies from the top batten strip down. Burnish the tape around the edges, and spray Engine Black on the roofs, taking care to thoroughly cover the area around the fan shrouds, exhaust stacks, and other details. Once you're satisfied, use the hair drier again.

Remove the masking tape, pulling the tape back sharply across itself. One nice feature of schemes like this—you don't need to worry if a bit of paint creeps under the tape, as the stripes between the colors hide any overlap.

Applying decals

There's plenty of decal striping on these models, but if you do it one side at a time, applying it becomes a manageable task. Review the section on stripes in Chapter 4 as a refresher.

One hint—never apply decals if you're tired or jumpy. Find something else to do. I also never work on decals (particularly stripes) for more than 45 minutes without taking a short break to walk around or work on another project.

Since I'm right-handed, I begin applying decals at the upper-left side of each shell. This reduces the chance of wrecking a wet decal by bumping it as I work across the model.

Start with the single yellow stripe on the upper batten strip. Cut the decal from the sheet and let it soak in the water. Use a brush to apply some water on the shell. Lift the stripe from the water and use tweezers to carefully slide it off the backing paper into position. Take your time, and keep the decal wet as you work on it. Use tweezers to gently position the stripe. Sight along the side frequently to check the alignment, making sure that it's straight.

Once it's in position, use a brush to apply Micro Sol to the stripe. Don't brush the setting solution along the stripe—that could shove it out of alignment. Instead, touch the brush gently to the stripe, let the solution wick off the brush, and lift the brush straight up.

While that's drying, move to the middle double stripe. Since it's wider, this decal is easier to align. Continue adding the stripes, along with the large roadname and herald, until they're all in place. Do the same with one side of the B unit. You can also add number board decals while the A unit is on its side.

Let the decals dry overnight, then go back over the model and use a sharp hobby knife to poke any air bubbles under the decals. Reapply Micro Sol to these areas.

Curved nose stripes

The decal sheet includes the curved nose stripes in two pieces—one for each side, from the top of the nose all the way around to the cab ladder. Decals like this are much easier to work with if you divide each side into three pieces and apply them individually as shown in fig. 9-7.

Set the A unit upright and start with the piece on top of the nose. Since the decal is too long, compare it to the painted pattern on the nose and trim the end that forms a point behind the headlight.

Apply the stripe as you did the others, taking time to ensure that it's properly aligned. Add setting solution, then give each piece a few minutes to dry before adding the next. By carefully butting each stripe to the previous one, no seams should be visible.

While the A unit's upright, add the curved stripe across the roof.

Final decals and paint touch-up

Once you've eliminated all of the air bubbles on the big decals, add the builder's plates, silver kickplates, and small rear road numbers. Don't forget to add the small letter "F" decals to the lower stripe at the front of each unit.

When all of the decals have dried thoroughly, use a wet paintbrush to mop away any residue of decal glue.

The porthole frames on these locomotives were painted red. If I did these locomotives again, I would cut circular pieces of masking tape and apply them over the portholes before painting the shells maroon. Since I lacked this bit of foresight, I used the edge of a small paintbrush to carefully paint them Caboose Red.

Use a small brush and some Accu-Flex Soo Line Yellow to paint the anti-climber on the A unit nose.

Details and weathering

Brush-paint the various grab irons maroon, as shown in fig. 9-8. Install them, using CA to glue them in place from the inside of the shell.

Seal the decals with a clear overcoat. I used a 1:1 mix of Testor's Glosscote and Dullcote to give the locomotives a slight sheen. Allow this to dry overnight.

Weather the roofs of both units using light oversprays of Accu-Flex Grimy Black. I concentrated the spray around the exhaust stacks and fans, and then added a light coat to the whole roof and the upper part of the sides.

After you install Number 450 Kadee couplers into the coupler-mounting slots on both locomotives, add the clear plastic "glass" to the cab and portholes, then place the shells on the frames. Paint the windshield wipers silver and install them too.

I added some light weathering to the trucks, lower body, and couplers, including a light dusting of Grimy Black and a bit of Armor Sand. I

BILL OF MATERIALS: CGW F-UNITS

Accu-Flex paints
16-01 Engine Black
16-03 Grimy Black
16-08 Caboose Red
16-53 Erie Lackawanna Maroon
16-103 Armor Sand

Detail Associates
701 F A-unit details
702 F B-unit details

Kadee
450 couplers (2 pkgs.)

Microscale
Micro Set
Micro Sol
87-48 diesel builder's plate decals
87-593 Chicago Great Western diesel decals
87-594 CGW diesel stripe decals
87-793 E- and F-unit data and number boards

ShellScale decals
105 EMD insert number boards

Stewart Hobbies
F3 A unit
F3 B unit

wanted the locomotives to be fairly clean, but still look as though they'd been working.

That's it! You now have a beautiful set of F3s, and best of all, you did it yourself.

Fig. 9-7. Apply the curved stripe in three sections— it's much easier to handle. The separations aren't noticeable when the sections are butted together.

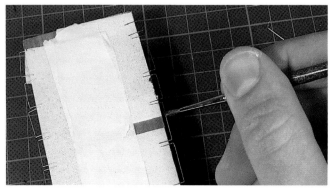

Fig. 9-8. Tape loops of masking tape to the edge of a board, then stick the various grab irons around the edge. Use a brush or airbrush to paint them maroon.

John C. Benson

10 Painting a Brass Diesel

Working in subassemblies to decorate a Union Pacific
Dash 8-40C

Brass locomotives are the jewels of model railroading. They're assembled by hand and made in small quantities, generally in Japan or Korea. They feature exquisite craftsmanship and are usually detailed to represent a specific locomotive or locomotive subclass.

Brass locomotives are also the single most expensive investment many modelers make. This, and the fact that brass isn't a common modeling medium, makes some modelers panic when confronted with the task of painting them.

However, you needn't worry. In many ways, brass models are easier to paint than plastic. You can usually divide them into several subassemblies, making it easier to paint multicolor schemes.

Brass models do present some challenges, but with a bit of time and patience you'll be able to create a paint job that enhances the craftsmanship of the model.

Prototype background

I chose to paint an HO scale brass General Electric Dash 8-40C from Overland Models. It's detailed to represent a locomotive in Union Pacific's initial Dash 8 order, nos. 9100–9174, which the railroad received in 1987.

The Union Pacific's Armour Yellow and Harbor Mist Gray is a popular scheme among modelers. It looks great on this modern diesel, which is rather amazing, considering that this basic scheme has been around since the

1940s! Because it's a two-color scheme with some striping, it is a challenge to paint and decal.

Preparing the model

I began by carefully removing the locomotive from the box. As fig. 10-1 shows, new brass models are usually well packaged in foam. This model had extra foam pieces protecting the handrails and other details. You'll want to save all of these packing materials.

Test the model by placing it on your layout or a test track and running it for a while in each direction to make sure that everything operates properly. If the mechanism needs work, now's the time to do it. Get the locomotive running the way you want before

Fig. 10-1. Carefully remove the model from its packing. The extra foam pieces protect the handrails and other details.

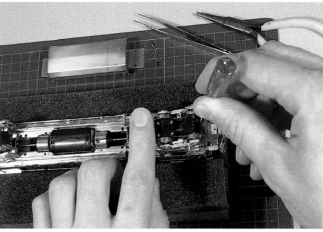

Fig. 10-2. Locate and remove the mounting screws. Make notes or drawings of any complicated or unusual fittings.

doing any detail and painting work.

This Overland model ran beautifully right away. Most brass models imported today are excellent runners, but this was not always the case. In the 1960s and '70s, brass models were chiefly designed as showpieces and not operational models. Consequently, many ran very poorly.

Be aware of this as you shop for a brass locomotive. There are plenty of used brass models available in hobby shops, through mail order outlets, and at dealers specializing in brass. The detail on many of these earlier models, while generally good, is also not up to today's standards. However, many older models have price tags that are quite attractive compared to new models, making them ideal as a first brass painting project.

Once everything's working, take the model to your workbench. You want to separate the model into as many subassemblies as possible. Most brass models are assembled with machine screws in hidden areas. Study the model to determine what each screw holds before taking it apart.

Most diesels such as this one are fairly simple. Figure 10-2 shows how the screws are usually hidden. A set of jeweler's screwdrivers, both standard and Phillips, is essential when working with brass models. Figure 10-3 shows the model after disassembly.

Be sure to keep track of the screws and where they belong. I used masking tape to stick all of the machine screws

to a piece of cardboard, then labeled each group. If you have a more complex model, or if you're afraid you'll forget before you get the model back together, take snapshots as you disassemble the model. You can also use drawings or a video camera to keep track of things.

Test-fit couplers in the coupler pockets. The model included mounting screws and the mounting holes were already tapped. I used a pair of Kadee no. 8 couplers on the Dash 8. To improve the look of these couplers, I used side-cutting pliers to cut off the uncoupling pins. Both of the mounting pads angled down toward the pilot openings, so I also used pliers to adjust them until they were level.

This model included etched-brass

plates that fit over the number boards. Although these should be attached with CA at this point, I forgot and had to add them after the model was painted—a touchy operation, to say the least.

The clear finish on this model was in good shape, with no chips, blobs, or runs, so I decided to spray the finish colors directly over it. Removing this finish can be difficult, so don't strip it unless it's absolutely necessary. If you have to strip it, or if the model is raw brass that has tarnished, check Chapter 3 for guidelines.

Scrub the parts with a toothbrush and dish detergent using warm water. Use an airbrush to blow away as much water as you can, then set the parts aside to dry.

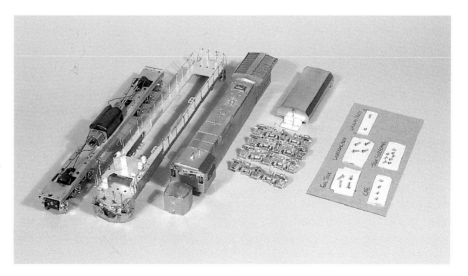

Fig. 10-3. Separate the model into as many pieces as possible for painting.

Fig. 10-4. Use quick bursts with the airbrush to get paint into all corners of the cab.

Fig. 10-5. Adding a light coat of the initial color helps seal the edges of the masking tape, preventing the second color from bleeding under.

Painting

Begin by painting the cab interior. I used a light green color that I mixed from Accu-Flex Reefer White and a few drops of dark green, just enough to turn the color.

Airbrush the interior as shown in fig. 10-4, making sure to coat each interior cab wall. When you're done, use a hair dryer for a minute to help cure the paint.

Cut pieces of masking tape to fit over the cab window openings from the inside, then add a wide piece of tape across the bottom of the cab opening.

The interior of each truck sideframe includes small plastic end caps for the axles. Leave these in place, but cover them with small squares of masking tape to keep paint out.

Airbrush the body, walkway assembly, nose, tank, and truck sideframes with Harbor Mist Gray. Use short, quick bursts to get paint into tight areas around the plows and pilots. Be sure to airbrush the truck sideframes from several angles to ensure complete coverage.

Both the walkway assembly and truck sideframes included chains. Be sure to cover them completely with paint, but don't allow them to rest on the model surface as they dry. You also need to be careful around screens. Spray them from several angles so that the mesh is completely coated, but don't apply so much paint that the tiny openings become filled.

Check each piece under a bright light to make sure there are no shiny brass parts shining through. As you finish each part, hold it under a hair dryer for a minute to help cure the paint.

Adding the yellow

Mask the cab base on the walkway assembly. Start with wide strips of masking tape pressed onto a sheet of glass and then cut into small pieces. The stanchions are all gray, including the areas on each side where they extend below the walkway. Use small strips of tape to mask these off.

Also mask the roof and upper sides of the body. I applied the mask so that the red decal stripe falls entirely on the gray area. This ensures that both red stripes are the same color. Use several small pieces of tape around details such as the cab sunshades and windshield wipers. Follow them with large pieces extending over the roof.

Burnish the tape along the painting edge. Then apply a light coat of gray around the edge as in fig. 10-5. This technique helps seal the tape, preventing the second color from bleeding under the edge. Again, cure this with a hair dryer, and you're ready to add the yellow.

Spray the Armour Yellow on the body, walkway, and nose. The yellow won't cover in one coat, so apply several light coats, but be sure that the paint is wet as it hits the surface. Dry each coat using a hair dryer.

Fig. 10-6. Use a brush to paint the corner handrails and other details. Masking tape helps keep stray paint from the body.

Be sure to paint in the corners behind the cab and around the large radiator fin on the rear. Also be sure to paint under the cab sunshades. Check the model under a bright light to make sure that the yellow is applied evenly.

When you're done, carefully peel the masking tape off of the body. Don't use a tweezers, knife, or other sharp object to get the tape started; you could scratch the paint. To free sticky areas, slide a wood toothpick with a chisel point under a corner of the tape.

The only airbrushing that's left to add is the dark gray anti-glare panel on the nose. Mask off the sides of the nose and spray Grimy Black on top. This color covers well, so one or two coats are all you'll need.

Brush-painting details

Unlike plastic models, most of the details are already in place on the body of a brass model, so it's usually necessary to do more detail and touch-up brush-painting.

I started by touching up a couple of areas where a bit of yellow crept under the tape. If some paint bleeds under, don't panic—touching it up with a brush will usually remove all traces, and the red decal stripe will also help to hide minor problems. Some yellow overspray also dusted a couple of areas on the handrails, so I gave them a coat of gray. I also touched up the gray stanchions where they extend down the yellow sides under the cab.

Paint the cab seats Engine Black. Give the control stand a wash of Polly S Engine Black, then paint silver on the gauges and control handles.

Paint the corner handrails white, as shown in fig. 10-6. A piece of masking tape under the handrails will prevent getting paint on the body. While you've got the white paint out, brush-paint the plow grab irons and ends of the uncoupling levers.

Use a fine-point brush to paint the m.u. and air hoses black. Next, add silver to the glad hands, and then brush-paint the grabs on top of the nose yellow. It will take a couple of coats for the yellow to cover well. Paint the wheel sides a rust color. For this I used Polly S Roof Brown and added a few streaks of Polly S Rust.

The gaskets around the windshields and cab-door windows are black. This is one of the toughest areas to paint on most models. The gaskets are raised slightly on the model, so I used the edge of a fine brush to carefully follow their outline.

If some black seeps over the gasket onto the surface, don't despair. Wait until it dries, then touch up the area with some yellow paint. Decal striping is a good alternative. Number-board gasket decals, such as those available from Microscale and others, can be cut to fit.

I mixed a few drops of Accu-Flex Santa Fe Silver and Primer Gray and used the mix to brush-paint the exhaust stack. Use red to paint the speed-recorder cable (on the right front truck sideframe) and various details near the fuel tank, then finish the detail painting by brushing a touch of silver on the windshield wipers and orange on the beacon.

Decals

The decal application is fairly simple. I used Microscale's set for modern UP diesels. Do one side of the body and walkway assembly at a time. One challenge of decorating brass models is that you must cut and fit decals around body details such as grab irons.

Start with the red striping—the wide stripe on the side sill and the narrow stripe on the body. Do the sill striping in segments, cutting each piece to fit between the stanchions. Trim each piece as close as possible to the stripe, as any excess clear material at the edge will make it difficult to align the stripe with the top of the walkway. Once the decal is in position, use a brush to add Micro Sol around the edges and let it dry.

Now do the same with the body stripe. Cut the pieces to fit around the windshield wipers, and end the stripe next to the cab sunshade as shown in the photos.

Continue decaling the large road name, cab numbers, and the numerous warning labels. The Microscale decal set includes a nice guide that shows the proper location for these small pieces.

After the decals dry, carefully use a sharp knife to pierce any air bubbles,

Fig. 10-7. Use a sharp hobby knife to poke any air bubbles under the decals, then reapply Micro Sol.

BILL OF MATERIALS: UP DASH 8-40C

Accu-Flex paints
16-01 Engine Black
16-02 Reefer White
16-03 Grimy Black
16-12 Primer Gray
16-24 Armour Yellow
16-25 Harbor Mist Gray
16-32 Santa Fe Silver

Detail Associates
1709 lenses

Evergreen styrene
9005 .005" clear sheet

Floquil
110004 Crystal Cote

Microscale
Micro Sol
Krystal Klear
87-523 Union Pacific modern diesel decals

Polly S paint
410010 Black
410070 Roof Brown
410073 Rust

ShellScale decal
117 modern number boards

then reapply the Micro Sol as shown in fig. 10-7.

Use the larger of the black number board backgrounds so that the entire board plus the gasket is covered. The decals aren't quite long enough, so I cut them in half, applied them, then added a thin filler strip cut from another number board (there are plenty of them on the sheet).

The number board numerals on the Microscale decal sheet don't quite match the style of the prototype either, so I substituted numerals from ShellScale set no. 117. Figure 10-8 shows the rear of the body, including the location of the red stripe and black number board borders.

Finish the decaling with the sill stripes on the ends and the UP herald on the nose, and then use a small piece of polyester foam dampened with water to clean up any areas where decal glue has smeared on the body. Check over the body thoroughly to make sure that all of the decals are in place and seated properly, and that you've touched up and painted everything.

Final details and reassembly

I wanted to model a new unit, and as the prototype photos show, the paint isn't flat—it has a satin sheen to it. To retain this effect I used a light coat of Floquil Crystal Cote.

Add "glass" to the cab interior with .005" clear styrene cut slightly larger than each opening, then glue it in place from behind using Micro Krystal Klear. Be sure you don't cover any of the

Fig. 10-8. This view shows the decal placement on the rear of the locomotive.

handrail openings in the cab sides. Also glue the Detail Associates headlight lenses in the openings.

I added a wash of Polly S Engine Black (1 part paint, 5 parts Polly S Airbrush Thinner) to all of the screens on each side of the body, as shown in fig. 10-9.

Small wire nubs extended from each of the m.u. sockets below the front anticlimber, so I added an m.u. cable made from wire insulation and painted it red. Cut these nubs off of the rear m.u. sockets, and then finish the cab

interior by using CA to glue a pair of Preiser seated figures to the cab seats as in fig. 10-10.

It's now time to put everything back together. Work carefully, going in reverse order from disassembly. When assembling the cab and body on the underframe, bend the handrails out at the cab so the handrail ends don't scrape the cab sides. Once the body is in place, bend the handrails back and insert the ends into the holes on the cab.

You can use these techniques to paint any brass diesel.

Fig. 10-9. Adding a thin black wash to the side screens helps provide an illusion of depth.

Fig. 10-10. A pair of seated figures adds life to the cab.

Northern no. 5632 was still going strong in 1963, albeit pulling fan trips instead of fast freight and passenger trains.

Jim Hediger

11 Painting a Brass Steam Engine

Techniques to paint and weather any brass or plastic steam locomotive

Painting steam locomotives, with their complex valve gear and often temperamental drive mechanisms, probably scares off more model railroaders than any other modeling project. However, like the other projects in this book, working on a steam engine isn't that tough if you take everything one step at a time.

Step by step you'll learn how to paint a brass steam locomotive, an HO scale Chicago, Burlington & Quincy O5-B 4-8-4 made in Korea by Daiyoung and imported by NJ International. The techniques are not specific to this locomotive—you can use these methods to paint almost any brass or plastic steam engine.

If you're not familiar with valve gear, rods, and other steam loco-

motive parts, it's helpful to do some research on the subject. Two good references are *Model Railroader Cyclopedia, Volume 1: Steam Locomotives* and *Guide to North American Steam Locomotives,* both available from Kalmbach Publishing Co. Both books offer diagrams of valve gear and cutaway views of locomotives, plus good information on how these machines work.

The model represents Burlington Route 4-8-4 (Northern) home-built locomotive nos. 5621-5635 as they appeared late in their careers with Mars lights on the nose and a signal box atop the boiler. The oil-burning locomotives in this series were classified O5-B to distinguish them from their O5-A coal-burning sisters.

Figure 11-1 shows the O5-B in all its prepainted splendor. As was common in the late 1970s when this model was made, the builder painted the model a gold color and then added a clear gloss finish. As I explained in Chapter 9, it's usually better to paint over a finish coat like this rather than trying to strip it. The finish on this model was in good shape, and wasn't too thick—something to watch for on brass models painted gold.

Disassembly

It's true with most painting projects, but especially with steam locomotives: painting is easy—it's the disassembly, preparation, and reassembly that take the most time and care.

Fig. 11-1. The builder painted this locomotive gold and added a clear gloss finish.

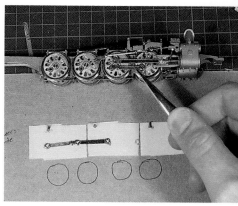

Fig. 11-2. Place these parts on masking tape in proper orientation to keep them in order.

Start by test-running the model. If there are any problems with the mechanism, or if you want to add weight to the boiler, upgrade the motor or drive line, or make any other modifications, now's the time to do it. It's a good idea to take photos of the model, including close-ups of the valve gear and underframe, for later reference when putting everything back together.

I disassembled the model O5-B in the following order: (Other steam locomotives will be similar, but variations in wheel arrangement, valve gear, and construction techniques may alter the sequence.)

Tender:
• Remove and disassemble trucks
• Remove floor.

Locomotive:
• Remove front truck (which also secures front of boiler)
• Remove rear mounting screws (on lower rear of cab connecting to frame)
• Lift boiler/cab from running gear
• Remove drawbar
• Remove and disassemble rear truck
• Remove pilot assembly
• Remove motor
• Disassemble and remove gearbox from driver
• Remove rods and valve gear
• Remove cylinder/crosshead guide assembly
• Remove valve gear hanger
• Remove cover to drivers
• Remove drivers.

As you progress through each step, make drawings to show how various pieces fit together. Undoubtedly, the most intimidating part of taking apart

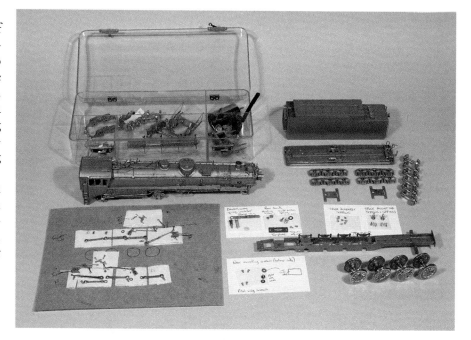

Fig. 11-3. Separating the model into as many parts as possible ensures a thorough painting job.

a steam locomotive is disassembling the valve gear and rods. Figure 11-2 shows how I placed the rods on masking tape attached to a sheet of cardboard. Use this method only if you're sure you'll be reassembling the model within a few weeks. Over time, masking tape will either lose its tackiness, leaving you with a collection of random parts, or become gooey, leaving residue on details.

Label each of the drivers as you remove them from the frame. I scribed small numbers at the rear of each one, then wrote the numbers on a card to keep track of them. Figure 11-3 shows the disassembled model. Plastic cases

divided into compartments are also great for keeping track of parts.

It is possible to paint the running gear, including wheels, rods, and valve gear, without disassembly. However, it's difficult to clean the parts thoroughly before painting.

Surface preparation

It's important to clean all of the parts before painting. My locomotive was typical of many brass imports (and many plastic models) in that it was grossly overlubricated. The wheels, rods, valve gear, and running gear were all coated with oil, some of which had transferred to the body. Clean all of this off and start from scratch.

Using a toothbrush, scrub all of the locomotive parts with dish detergent and warm water, then rinse with clean water. Repeat this for all parts of the running gear to ensure that all oil and grease is removed. Use an airbrush to blow away big drops of water, then set the parts aside to dry.

I cleaned the various rods and valve-gear parts one at a time, then placed them on a fresh piece of tape on their cardboard reference sheets. Don't clean the small parts in a sink with an open

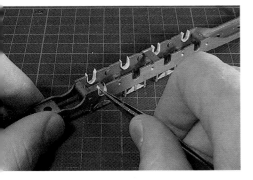

Fig. 11-4. Use small pieces of masking tape to cover the openings for the wheel bearings.

Fig. 11-5. Cover the openings for the ends of the axles.

Fig. 11-6. Buffing silver-plating powder over brass will leave a polished metal appearance.

drain—losing a part on a brass locomotive can be catastrophic. Use small bowls, one with detergent and water, the other with plain distilled water.

Several areas require masking on steam locomotives. Use small bits of masking tape to cover the notches in the frame that hold the wheel bearings, as shown in fig. 11-4. Use Magic Mask to cover the wheel ends on the locomotive trailing truck and tender wheelsets. Masking tape will cover the journals on the inside of the truck sideframes, as in fig. 11-5. Add pieces of masking tape over the tender kingpin, driver crankpins, and the tender truck bolsters. As you add masking, avoid touching the model with your bare fingers—use painting handles or wear a pair of latex rubber gloves.

The crosshead guides should be a natural metal color, and should have a smooth, polished surface for the crossheads to slide on. On many models these parts are nickel-plated, but on this one they're brass and painted in the same gold paint and clear finish as the rest of the model.

If you encounter this situation, use a hobby knife to scrape the finish from

the guides until you're down to bare brass. Scrubbing with lacquer thinner may also help remove the finish. Be careful not to bend or break the guides from the cylinders, though.

Plate the guides using Detail Associates silver-plating powder. Using it is easy: with a piece of damp cloth, rub the powder along the brass surface as shown in fig. 11-6, and in a minute you'll have a polished, natural-metal surface. Do this before cleaning the parts, not after painting (as I did).

Painting

I airbrushed the locomotive and tender with Floquil paint, using a mix of 2 parts Engine Black and 1 part Grimy Black. This mix looks black, but is light enough to show details and highlights.

Mix 3 parts paint with 1 part thinner, set the pressure to 16 pounds, and test the spray on a piece of scrap material. While painting, I used a GB Engineering handle to hold the locomotive and tender shells. I used tweezers to hold the other parts or else stuck them on loops of masking tape attached to pieces of cardboard.

The enclosed vestibule cab on the CB&Q engine made it difficult to paint the cab interior, but you can manage to cover most areas by spraying through the rear door and cab windows. Use short bursts and aim into the corners.

Spray the boiler from several angles to ensure good coverage around all the piping and details. When you're done there, airbrush the tender, tender floor, tender and locomotive truck sideframes, pilot, valve gear hanger, and cylinder assembly. I used the jig in fig. 11-7 to hold the wheelsets for painting.

Let the parts dry for 24 hours, then add a coat of Floquil Crystal Cote, mixed 3:1 with Floquil Airbrush Thinner for spraying. Crystal Cote provides a gloss surface that is a good base for decals and will show some sheen when the locomotive is completed. Let the gloss coat dry for 24 hours.

"But wait—shouldn't steam locomotives be painted with a flat finish?" you ask. As I explained in Chapter 6, prototype steam locomotives often wore glossy paint. Finishes varied quite a bit

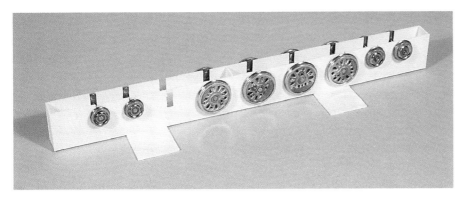

Fig. 11-7. A simple box made from styrene with slots works well to hold wheels for painting.

among eras and railroads depending on use and weathering, so check photos of the prototype you're modeling.

Adding a second color

Many railroads painted smokeboxes and fireboxes with a graphite-and-oil mixture, which has a dark, silvery sheen. Others painted smokeboxes silver or gray. Once again, check prototype photos. I started with a mix of 3 parts Floquil Old Silver and 1 part Graphite. This turned out brighter than I wanted, but I toned it down later with some weathering.

Mask these areas as shown in figs. 11-8 and 11-9. Take your time and be careful around the delicate piping and details.

Airbrush the graphite mixture on the smokebox and firebox. Use light coats—the silver mix covers well, and there's no need to cover details by applying excessive paint. Remove the masking as shown in fig. 11-10, then let the paint dry overnight.

Use a brush to touch up any black areas on the front as shown in figs. 11-11 and 11-12, then paint the handrail, bell, headlights, and classification lights.

While you're waiting for paint on the boiler to dry, you can paint the rods and valve gear. Treatment of these pieces varied among railroads, so again, refer to photos before painting your model.

Photos of the 5632 from the late '50s showed that the side rods, main rod, and eccentric rod were a natural weathered metal color. I placed these parts on some masking tape and airbrushed them with an Accu-Flex mix of 1 part Grimy Black and 1 part Primer Gray. This turned out much too bright, but it will be toned down later with some weathering.

The rest of the valve gear is black, so I brush-painted it with the Floquil black mix.

Cab roof

Steam locomotive cab roofs (and tender decks) were prone to rusting, so many railroads painted them an oxide red color to conceal the rust. Color photos of the 5632 showed its cab roof painted this way, so I used masking tape and paper to mask the rest of the locomotive. I airbrushed the roof with Accu-Flex Light Tuscan Oxide Red, then removed the masking.

Reassembling the running gear

If taking a steam locomotive apart is the scariest modeling adventure, then putting it back together ranks second. However, if you've taken good notes (literally) you'll be surprised at how easy it is. Start with the running gear, and replace parts in the reverse order of the way they were disassembled.

Once you get the valve gear and rods back in place, roll the engine back and forth to make sure there's no binding. Add a small drop of light oil to each driver bearing, then add a drop of oil inside the gearbox before remounting it and the motor.

Finally, use a brush and black paint to cover up the screwheads holding the side rods in place.

Decals

Use Champion set no. EH-20 for Burlington steam locomotives, and set HD-33D for the tender data and "O5B" lettering on the cab. Champion Decal Set works well for adhering the decals to the surface.

The front number board, which has a Dulux Gold border and matching numbers, is the toughest part of lettering this model. The Champion set included the numbers, but nothing for the border. I considered painting it, but then decided to try decaling it instead. I used a piece of Microscale Dulux

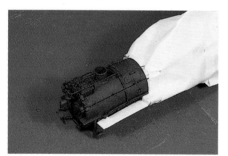
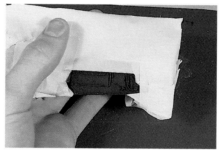

Figs. 11-8 and 11-9. Use small pieces of tape to get around the piping and other details, then use larger pieces of tape and paper to finish the job.

Figs. 11-11 and 11-12. Brush-paint handrails, headlight, bell, and other parts on the front.

Fig. 11-10. Pull the tape back sharply across itself as you remove it.

Fig. 11-13. Mask the area that will be the number face (I did several just to be sure), then airbrush the sheet black.

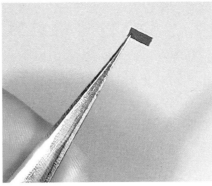

Fig. 11-14. Remove the tape, then trim the decal with a narrow Dulux Gold border.

Gold trim film, as shown in figs. 11-13 and 11-14. Apply it to the number board like a regular decal.

Once the decals are dry, add a coat of Crystal Cote over the lettering and let the model dry for 24 hours.

Weathering

Decide how much weathering you want to add to the model. If you're going to weather it, it's easier to do the running gear and boiler before you reassemble them.

I wanted a locomotive that appeared grimy from use, but not one that was overly filthy. I started by drybrushing grimy black on the smokebox sides, streaking the color down from the stack, around the various pipes and fittings. I also added some drybrushed streaks on the boiler sides and on the sides and rear of the tender.

Cut small pieces of masking tape to cover the number boards on the smokebox front.

Mix a batch of "dirty black" and thin it for airbrushing. I use a mix of 1 part Polly S Engine Black, 1 part Grimy Black, and about 10 parts Airbrush Thinner. Spray this mix around the smokebox, down the boiler and tender sides over the drybrushed areas, around the exposed part of the firebox, and on the bottom of the cab. Some of the gloss black areas show through this weathering, adding some nice contrast.

When weathering the drivers and rods with an airbrush, it helps to have the locomotive running so that the weathering goes on evenly. Figure 11-15 shows how I did it. I set the

mechanism on a piece of track in the spray booth and clipped a pair of wires from a power pack to the motor. I turned on the power and held the frame with one hand and airbrushed the sides with the other. Use both the thinned dirty black mix and thinned Polly S Earth.

Cover any exposed parts of the motor or gearbox with tape to avoid getting paint where it shouldn't be. When you finish, use a pipe cleaner dipped in lacquer thinner to clean the wheel treads, being careful not to touch the wheel sides.

Window glazing

On many steam locomotives the rear of the cab is completely open, making it fairly easy to add windows. The O5-B isn't one of them. The model's vestibule cab allows limited access to the cab interior, making it difficult to add glazing.

Clear .005" styrene is easy to work with and works well in most applications. I used it for both side windows, gluing it from inside with Microscale Micro Krystal Klear. The model has its sliding windows in the forward position so the rear part of the main openings are open with no glazing.

I tried several times to get pieces of styrene into the narrow front windows (alongside the boiler), but the narrow space and uneven interior surface made it nearly impossible. I finally resolved to leave them open and hope no one notices!

Microscale Krystal Klear was my solution to glazing the small windows at the rear of the cab sides. Krystal Klear resembles white glue. To use it, apply it from behind by placing a large blob of it above the top of the opening. Use a flat stick to pull it down over the opening, making it form a bubble across the opening. I used a paper clip bent into an L shape to reach into the open large cab window and apply the Krystal Klear from behind.

Final details

Put the tender back together, and add the boiler to the running gear. Place the locomotive and tender on the track and test-run it to make sure all is well.

Add the headlight and classification-light lenses using various-sized lenses from MV Products.

CB&Q Northern no. 5632 is now ready to head the next fast freight Everywhere West out of Chicago!

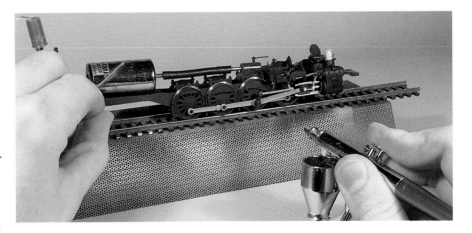

Fig. 11-15. Airbrushing the running gear while it's in motion ensures even coverage. When done the rods will be a lighter shade of grime than the wheels.

12 Painting Structures
A coat of paint will improve the realism of any kit

Structures tell a lot about a model railroad. By looking at the types of structures, building styles, signs, and weathering, you can get clues about where a town is located and what era the modeler is trying to re-create.

There's a tremendous variety of structure kits on the market, including mass-produced (and relatively inexpensive) injection-molded styrene kits, wood and plaster craftsman kits, urethane kits, and laser-cut wood kits that go together quite easily.

When you're considering a structure kit, look beyond the shiny plastic and bare wood and try to picture what it will look like when you're done. The photos on many plastic kit boxes are, to say the least, unattractive. However, some paint and a few decals can transform even a marginal kit into an attractive scenic item.

We'll build two HO scale structures from start to finish.

BRICK DRUGSTORE

Let's start with a basic injection-molded styrene kit. This corner brick building from Bachmann has good molded brick detail, nice cornice and window header detail, and an interesting shape that sets it apart from others. You can, of course, use these same techniques on almost any brick structure kit.

The kit has separate walls, and the cornice and window headers are separate castings, which makes painting a bit easier. Begin by trimming all of the parts (except for the window and door castings) from their sprues. Clear any flash with a hobby knife.

Build the structure into subassemblies for painting, as in fig. 12-1. First, glue the walls and base together. Assemble the chimney and walls for the rooftop doorway. Glue the cornice together, and then attach the window headers and footings to a piece of card with masking tape as the photo shows. Add a strip of masking tape around the

smooth areas at the tops of the two front sides where the cornice will go.

Using thin strips of masking tape, cover the edges of the window and door frames as shown in fig. 12-2. After airbrushing them (I used Accu-Flex Reefer White), remove the tape.

Brick and mortar

Brick buildings come in a nearly infinite variety of colors, from various shades of red and maroon to tan and brown. Mortar ranges from light gray to many darker colors, and in many cases is mixed to match the brick color.

Fig. 12-1. Assemble the building into subassemblies for painting.

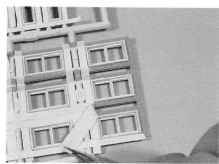

Fig. 12-2. Mask the window frames with strips of masking tape before painting. This will make gluing them easier.

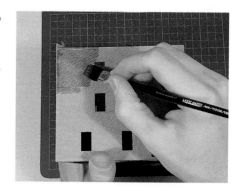

Fig. 12-3. Use a wide, flat brush to pat the brick color onto the brick surface. Don't use conventional brush strokes, or the red paint will get in the mortar lines.

Many brick buildings are painted, giving the mortar lines the same color as the structure. It's almost impossible to be "wrong" when it comes to color. If you're having problems choosing colors, take a look at a few prototype brick buildings for ideas.

The method I used to re-create mortar lines may look radical, but it's one of the best—and easiest—techniques I've seen. It works especially well for structures with deep mortar lines such as this one.

Begin by painting the building the mortar color, which can be nearly any shade of gray. I airbrushed the store with a coat of Accu-Flex Primer Gray, making sure the paint got into the mortar lines.

Once this dries, use a wide flat brush to apply the brick color, as shown in fig. 12-3. I used Accu-Flex Light Tuscan Oxide Red. Don't let the brush get too wet—the key is to keep the brush fairly dry and use the flat side of the brush to pat the brick color on

Other ways to create mortar

One of the most popular ways to create mortar is to flow a wash of thinned water-base white or gray paint over a wall. This tends to settle in mortar lines, but often spreads out over the brick surface as it dries. When the paint starts to dry, wipe the brick surface with a damp cloth and the mortar color will remain in the cracks. This method takes some practice, but generally works well.

Another technique is to use compounds such as Modeler's Mortar or Roberts Brick Mortar Formula. These are water-based paints designed to be spread on the brick surface, then wiped away after they dry.

the brick surface without getting paint in the mortar lines. Figures 12-4 and 12-5 show the results.

At this point the mortar lines were a bit too prominent for the effect I

wanted. The next step allows nearly infinite control over the mortar color. Load the airbrush with thinned brick color (I used 1 part red to 2 parts water) and set the airbrush for a very light spray. Airbrush the structure with this mix until you have the effect you're looking for, as in figs. 12-4 and 12-5. Remove the masking tape from the top of the walls.

You can stop at this point and have a very convincing brick effect, but I decided to go one step further. I wanted this structure to have the varied effect of multi-toned bricks, which are often seen in prototype structures of this type.

With a fine-point brush and some Accu-Flex Dark Tuscan Oxide Red, I began painting individual bricks at random, as shown in figs. 12-6 and 12-7. This looked as though it would take forever, but when done a bit at a time it wasn't nearly as difficult as I had thought. I only did the two front walls, figuring that the rear walls will eventually be hidden by adjoining buildings.

Fig. 12-4. To blend the stark gray mortar color, airbrush the walls lightly with a thinned mix of the brick color.

Fig. 12-5. Here you can see the improved appearance after misting the brick.

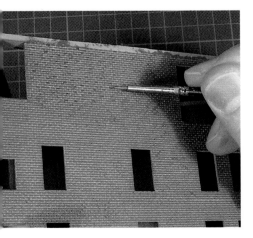

Figs. 12-6 and 12-7. Use a fine-point brush to paint individual bricks various shades of red. Take care not to get paint in the mortar lines.

Fig. 12-8. Use a mix of Polly S Black and Grimy Black on the roof.

Fig. 12-9. Once the sign is painted, use a knife to scrape paint off of the raised plastic letters.

Fig. 12-10. Use .020" styrene to make window displays. They make the structure look "busy" and help hide the lack of interior detail.

Using a 1:1 mix of the light and dark reds, I painted more bricks for some additional variety. The brush-painted bricks dried with a bit of a sheen, so I airbrushed the whole structure with a light coat of Testor's Dullcote.

Detail painting

Airbrush the cornice and window pieces with a light gray mix of Polly S paints. I started with an ounce of Reefer White, then added drops of Concrete until the color started to change. I then added drops of Earth in the same way. Mix this 3:2 with Polly S Airbrush Thinner for spraying.

The roof has some nice molded details. On a textured roof, brush marks do no harm. I brush-painted it as shown in fig. 12-8, using the brush to mix the black and grimy black as I painted.

Paint the skylight and the roof for the stairway black. Since the skylight was molded in red plastic, it's easier to paint it, figuring that the windows had been boarded up and painted over.

Putting it together

Glue the cornice in place around the top of the front walls and glue the window trim in place. I used a chisel-point knife to scrape away the paint above and below the windows before gluing, but if I did this project again, I'd probably use small pieces of tape to mask these areas before painting.

Glue the doors and double-hung windows in place, making sure that the windows are right-side-up. Add .005" clear styrene "glass" to the display windows and front door, then glue these pieces in place. I had to use white paint to touch up a couple of spots where the frames meet.

Signs

The kit included signs, but they weren't very realistic, so I decided to create my own. I decided to use a projecting sign on the short-wall side and a wall-mounted flat sign on the long side.

Walthers no. 933-3136 sign kit includes some great projecting sign blanks in different shapes and styles. I chose a tall one, as shown in the photo of the finished structure. I created the "DRUGS" sign at the bottom using raised plastic letters (Slater's 3mm), but you can also use dry transfers or decals.

If you use the plastic letters, secure them by using a brush to dab a bit of liquid plastic cement on the sign face. Use tweezers to set each letter in place, then maneuver it into position. Add more cement once the letter is in place.

Once the glue dries, paint the sign. I airbrushed it with Accu-Flex C&NW Green, with a few drops of white added to lighten the color. Use a chisel-tip knife to scrape the paint off the top of the plastic letters as shown in fig. 12-9.

The tall "LENZEN" is dry-transfer lettering. I burnished it to plain decal

Fig. 12-11. A piece of black construction paper keeps people from looking all the way through the building.

paper, then applied it like a regular decal. The Coca-Cola sign is from Microscale decal set no. 87-197.

I used the sign plate that came with the kit for the wall-mounted sign. The 7-Up decal is from Microscale set no. 87-197 and the "LENZEN DRUGS" was constructed from dry transfers and blank decals, as was the vertical sign.

I made window boxes as shown in fig. 12-10, then painted them and added paper cutouts from an NEB&W Green Dot sign and graphic set. It's not necessary to decorate the whole interior of a building—simply adding a few details in the windows adds life and makes the building more interesting.

I made the paper signs across the top of the display windows with a computer and laser printer, but you can also use dry-transfer letters. Several companies make nice color advertising signs, and I put a few of them in the windows. The window shades are pieces of manila file folders glued in place from behind.

Final details

To keep viewers from seeing directly through the building, I added a black construction paper view block as shown in fig. 12-11. This piece also hides the lack of interior detail.

The drug store is now ready to install on a layout. By using various paint colors, signs, and decals, you can start with simple kits and create several blocks of distinctive buildings that are unique to your layout.

These Microscale HO and N scale decal sets are just a few of the signs on the market today.

Signs

While some structure kits include signs, I like to create my own. It adds a personal touch, making the structure different from the thousands of other identical kits.

When making signs, I like to either re-create ones that exist in real life or make up names that immortalize friends. The first is a good way to establish the location or prototype of your layout; the latter is a great way to say "thanks" to people who've helped with the layout (perhaps naming an electrical shop after someone who has worked on your wiring).

Signs can also be a way to show your sense of humor, with subtle (or not-so-subtle) puns, jokes, or twists of names. However, even the funniest jokes can grow stale if you see them every day.

The Lenzen Drugs building shows one way of combining various commercial dry-transfer and decal alphabet sets. Alphabet sets are available in a tremendous variety of styles and sizes. Microscale makes several decal sign sets that can be used as is or combined with other graphics.

Other good sources include stationery, matchbook covers, magazine ads, and promotional brochures. You can create distinctive signs by combining several of these elements. Many companies make full-color advertising signs that are reproductions of real ones.

If you own or have access to a computer, you can create signs and print them on paper or acetate to create various effects. If you can use a color printer, you have even more options available. Otherwise, you can use watercolors to add color to single-color printouts.

Creating painted-on signs

Look in any downtown or older industrial area and you'll find dozens of examples of signs that have been painted on brick structures. Some are essentially

Look above the modern billboards on this corner structure and you'll see the weathered remains of several old painted-on signs. Even if you model the modern era, you can legitimately sneak some old-time advertising signs onto your structures.

billboards or advertisements, while others proudly display company names. Since railroads typically go through the older parts of cities where these are prevalent, most layouts can use some signs like this.

Fortunately they are easy to create by using dry transfers as masks, and the results look great. Here's how I made the Berghoff Beer sign on a brick store:

Start by painting the background area the desired color for the lettering (white for the beer sign). Place the dry transfers on the building and burnish them lightly. Use just enough pressure so that they leave the transfer paper and stick to the surface as shown in figs. 12-19 and 12-20. I added mask-

ing tape around the edge of the beer sign to give it a white border.

Airbrush the background color over the area. Apply very light coats so the paint doesn't creep under the dry transfers. When the paint dries, use masking tape to remove the dry transfers as shown in fig. 12-21. The result is a sign that looks as though it's been painted on. To make the Berghoff sign look as though it had been there awhile, I airbrushed it lightly with the color I'd used for the bricks.

The Berghoff lettering is from a Clover House set for a billboard reefer. Clover House has dozens of sets like this that would make great advertising signs. You can also use alphabet sets to create any number of these signs.

Figs. 12-19 and 12-20. Burnish the lettering using only enough pressure to get the transfers to stick on the wall.

Figs. 12-21 and 12-22. Masking tape will remove the dry transfers, leaving a painted-on sign.

WOOD INTERLOCKING TOWER

Wood kits have been around since the start of the hobby. Many of them, such as the fine kits from Campbell, FineScale Miniatures, and others, fall into the craftsman category. They usually require quite a bit of cutting and fitting.

This kit from American Model Builders features laser-cut wood parts that interlock and fit together with no trimming, with construction similar to plastic kits. A structure from this line of kits is a great (and simple) way to play with some techniques for finishing wood.

First, determine the colors you want to use for your structure. I decided to paint the interlocking tower white with oxide red stairs and a black roof.

As with any other building, it's best to paint things in subassemblies. Start with the windows, as shown in fig. 12-12. Put them together for painting, but leave off the glazing. Do the same with the doors.

Peeling paint

I wanted a tower that looked as though it was in need of a paint job but was still in decent shape. The wood siding of this kit afforded a perfect opportunity to create the effect of peeling paint. You can use this technique to create anything from a couple of subtle patches to an entire wall where the paint is barely hanging on.

Start by staining the wood as shown in fig. 12-13. I used a thin wash of black paint (Polly S Engine Black thinned with about 6 parts Polly S Airbrush Thinner). Follow it with a bit of Grimy Black drybrushing. You don't have to do this to the entire wall—only the areas where you want the paint to peel.

Stain the upper floor at the same time. Figure 12-14 shows one problem you will encounter when staining wood—the floor has warped slightly.

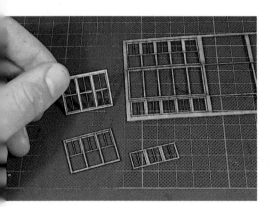

Fig. 12-12. Assemble the windows as much as possible before painting.

Fig. 12-13. Stain the walls only in the areas where you want to re-create peeling paint.

Fig. 12-14. Stain the floor to keep people from looking in and seeing bright wood.

On a small structure like this it's usually not a big problem, but on larger structures it's wise to brace walls from behind with ¼" square stripwood to prevent warping.

Open a bottle of rubber cement (it must be fresh, so to be safe, use a new bottle). Dip a brush in the cement and streak it onto the wall surface where you want the paint to peel, as shown in fig. 12-15. You can paint large patches or use a fine-point brush to touch small areas.

Wait approximately five minutes, then apply the wall paint. I used Accu-Flex Reefer White, applied with an airbrush. Paint the windows at the same time (unless you've picked another color for the trim) along with the trim strips.

Let the paint dry for approximately 30 minutes, then scrub the walls with a pencil eraser as shown in fig. 12-16, to remove the rubber cement. Don't be afraid to rub hard—the eraser has the added benefit of dulling the paint surface and creating its own subtle weathering effects.

I finished the white pieces by adding a very thin black wash over everything as shown in fig. 12-17. You can vary this wash to produce the weathered effect you're looking for. Finish assembling the structure according to the instructions.

Final details

Paint all of the parts for the stairway. I airbrushed them Accu-Flex Light Tuscan Oxide Red. Figure 12-18 shows how I used the rubber-cement technique again on the stair treads, creating some wear where feet have stepped most often. Finish assembling the stairway, and use a brush to touch up any areas that need it.

I brush-painted the roof with a 1:1 mix of Accu-Flex Flat Black and Grimy Black, then painted the underside of the roof white.

Once again, you can use these techniques on any structure to create weathering effects from mild to severe.

Fig. 12-15. Streak the rubber cement onto the wall where you want the paint to peel.

Fig. 12-16. Use a pencil eraser to remove the rubber cement.

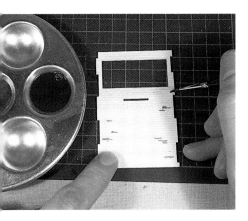

Fig. 12-17. A thin black wash helps tone down the stark white walls.

Fig. 12-18. Use the rubber-cement technique to create signs of wear on the stair treads.

13 Bridges and Trestles
Painting truss and plate-girder bridges and a wood trestle

Railroads paint their steel bridges in a variety of different colors, but the most common are black, silver, and oxide red.

As the prototype photos show, natural weathering often creates dramatic effects on these structures. Since bridges often go for years between paint jobs, weathering the bridges on your layout is almost a necessity. The first step in creating a realistic bridge is to visualize what kind of an effect you want before you begin painting.

Through truss

It's a good idea to paint a bridge like this in subassemblies. Painting these lacy structures with anything but an airbrush or aerosol can is difficult. Spray painting is the only way to get an even coat of paint into all of the model's nooks and crannies.

On this bridge I wanted to try something new—a radical technique I learned from Randy Pepprock, owner of Downtown Deco and a former Hollywood set builder.

This Walthers HO scale double-track through truss bridge was molded in dark gray plastic, a good base color for this technique. If you have a bridge molded in a lighter color, paint it grimy black or dark gray as you assemble it.

Once you have assembled the bridge completely, use a spray can of Floquil Rail Brown to paint patches of the bridge. Figure 13-1 shows how mine looked when I was done. Use short, quick bursts—remember, with spray cans you get a lot of paint coming out in a hurry. Make your coverage very light in some areas and heavy in others—this will add contrast when the bridge is done. Let the paint dry overnight.

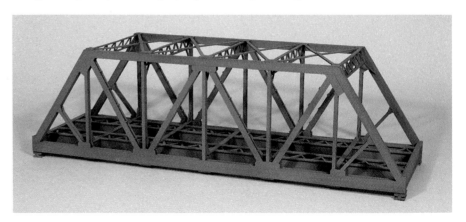

Fig. 13-1. Spray the completed bridge with Floquil Rail Brown to provide an underlying rust color.

76

Fig. 13-2. Use a trigger spray bottle to mist the bridge with water.

Fig. 13-3. While the bridge is wet, use an aerosol can of Floquil Engine Black to spray the entire structure.

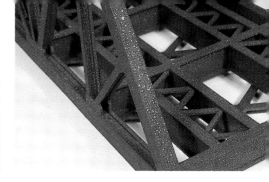

Fig. 13-4. The water acts as a mask to keep the black from covering completely, leaving patches of the Rail Brown showing through.

Now comes the radical part. Use a spray bottle to mist the bridge with water as shown in fig. 13-2. The water will act as a mask so the final color won't cover completely, leaving patches of rust showing through.

Now, with the water on the model, use a spray can of Engine Black to paint the bridge. Use short bursts and try to cover the entire bridge. When you're about half or two-thirds done, spray more water onto the bridge, then finish painting as in fig. 13-3. Spray even more water onto the bridge, then set it aside to dry overnight.

When everything's dry the bridge will look something like fig. 13-4. The effect is that of a black bridge with patches of rust showing through. In many areas the black will appear to be rusting off.

I then finished the bridge by adding a grimy black weathering spray in a few areas, along with some drybrushed grime and rust colors. I also used some real rust by painting small patches with Roof Brown, then dusting on rust powder scraped from an old railroad spike while the paint was still wet.

The water-spray technique can also be used on vehicles, structures, freight cars, and many other applications. You can apply a very light mist of water for subtle effects, or you can drench the model for some heavy-duty deterioration.

You can use any combination of colors to achieve different effects. The key is to use a lacquer-based paint for the final coat, so that the paint and water will repel each other.

You'll want to paint the track by airbrushing the sides of the rails with Accu-Flex Milwaukee Road Brown. Airbrush the ties by spraying straight down on the track with Accu-Flex Flat Black.

Add the track to the bridge, and the bridge will be ready to install on your layout.

Bridge abutments

The abutments for the truss and plate-girder bridges are Magnuson Models polyester resin castings. They're made to simulate concrete and include horizontal mold-board effects.

Begin by airbrushing them a concrete color. I used Polly S paint, starting with Reefer White, then adding Concrete and Earth until the color started to change. You can adjust this mix to achieve a number of effects. New, fresh concrete is almost white. As it ages, concrete turns gray and tan.

Fig. 13-5. Add vertical drybrushed streaks of various rust colors to the abutments.

Fig. 13-6. Airbrush thinned rust and black colors to tie the weathering together.

Fig. 13-7. Water creates horizontal marks on piers, as shown on this Soo Line bridge in Sebula, Iowa. You can re-create this effect with drybrushing, washes, or sprays.

The prototype photos show how rust from bridges washes down and stains abutments. Figure 13-5 shows how to replicate this by drybrushing various rust colors, including Roof Brown, Rust, and orange. These stains most often appear under the bridge feet but can also appear on other areas.

Using an airbrush, add highlights with thinned rust and black colors. Figure 13-6 shows the finished abutments.

Most weathering effects on abutments and piers are vertical. Piers in water are an exception, as fig. 13-7 shows. You can re-create this by drybrushing weathering colors horizontally or by masking the pier horizontally before airbrushing.

When weathering piers in water, be sure to keep the high-water mark even across all of the piers. Also, be sure that the high-water mark isn't above the nearby river banks.

Plate-girder bridge

Deck and through plate-girder are the most common railroad bridges. Since they're open, it's usually easy to paint them after assembly. If possible, add the ties and track after the bridge is completely painted. That way you can paint and weather the track separately, as you did with the truss bridge.

Since I had already assembled this Central Valley double-track bridge, I started by masking the ties on each deck.

I wanted to capture the overall look of the prototype bridge in fig. 13-8, but I didn't want to weather it too much.

Start by painting the underlying (rust) color first, just as you did with the truss bridge. Figure 13-9 shows how I sprayed Floquil Rail Brown (from an aerosol can) vertically on the sides. Let it dry for a couple of days.

The final color of the bridge is silver, so I airbrushed Polly S Flat Aluminum (a good dull silver color) on the bridge bottom. Spray it vertically on the sides, applying it lightly and letting some of the Rail Brown show through, as in fig. 13-10. Let it dry overnight.

I added a C&NW decal from a Herald King set to the side. Finish the weathering by drybrushing streaks of various rust and grime colors on the sides. Follow this with a light airbrush

Fig. 13-8. This Chicago & North Western bridge started out silver, but streaks of oxide-red primer and rust are showing through.

Fig. 13-9. Start with an underlying coat of Floquil Rail Brown.

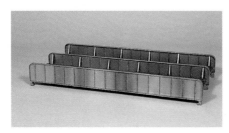

Fig. 13-10. Use vertical strokes to airbrush silver on the girders. Let some of the Rail Brown show through.

This lacy bridge in Oshkosh, Wisconsin, is showing signs of age, with multicolored rust patches dominating an aging coat of black paint.

coat of grimy black, then a light coat of Testor's Dullcote to seal the weathering.

Timber trestle

Modelers seem to love towering wood trestles because they make dramatic scenes on layouts. These huge structures are tough to find on prototype railroads these days, but small wood pile trestles such as the one in fig. 13-11 can be found on main lines across the country.

Nothing looks as much like wood as wood. Yes, it's possible to make trestles from plastic, but it's hard to capture the varied shading and grain of real wood.

The creosote-treated lumber used in trestles varies greatly in appearance. Depending on the type of treatment, type of wood, and length of time it's had to weather, the wood color can range from light gray to brown to black.

A great way to re-create this look is by staining the wood with thinned paint. Staining lets the natural wood grain show through, making each piece unique. By building up the paint in thin layers of different colors, it's possible to obtain any number of effects.

It's important to stain all the wood

before assembly. If any glue gets on the surface of the wood during assembly it will dry clear, but will repel stain.

A small trestle is the perfect project for experimenting with wood-staining techniques. I built mine from a T. P. Fleming kit.

Start by mixing stains using burnt umber, raw umber, and Mars Black artist's tube acrylics. Squeeze some paint into a paint tray or small cup, then add water.

Use a small stick to stir the paint, but don't mix it thoroughly. That way

you can vary the effects by reaching down to the bottom with your brush to get a thicker paint mix.

Start by staining the wood with the burnt umber as shown in fig. 13-12. Vary the effect among the pieces, and add occasional highlights with raw umber. The effects will usually appear dark when first applied and then lighten as the paint dries.

Now stain the pieces with black, as in fig. 13-13. Once again, vary the effects. Let the pieces dry for a day, then assemble the trestle.

Fig. 13-12. Use burnt umber as a base, adding highlights of raw umber.

Fig. 13-13. Finish with a black stain, varying the intensity among the pieces from black to light gray.

Fig. 13-11. This double-track trestle on the Santa Fe main line near Ancona, Illinois, serves dozens of trains a day.

Appendix
Addresses of companies listed in this book

Decal and dry-transfer manufacturers

Accu-cals, SMP Industries, 63 Hudson Rd., P. O. Box 72, Bolton, MA 01740: HO scale decals for northeastern U.S. and Canadian railroads.

CDS Lettering Ltd., P. O. Box 78003 Cityview, Nepean, Ontario K2G 5W2: N, HO, S, and O scale dry transfers for North American Railroads, with an emphasis on Canada.

Champion Decal Co., P. O. Box 1178, Minot, ND 58702: HO and O scale decals for North American railroads, specializing in steam and early diesel eras.

Clover House, P. O. Box 62, Sebastopol, CA 95473-0062: N, HO, S, and O scale dry transfers for turn-of-the-century through late-steam-era railroads.

Herald King, Miller Advertising, P. O. Box 1133, Bettendorf, IA 52722: HO scale decals for North American railroads.

Microscale Industries, P. O. Box 11950, Costa Mesa, CA 92627: N, HO, S, O, and G scale decals for North American railroads.

Oddballs Custom Decals, 26550 227th St., McLouth, KS 66054: N and HO scale diesel-era decals for U.S. railroads.

ShellScale Decals, 2140 Houston Mines Rd., Troutville, VA 24175: HO scale number board decals and N, HO, and O scale decals for Norfolk Southern and predecessors.

Wm. K. Walthers, P. O. Box 18676, Milwaukee, WI 53218: N, HO, and O scale decals for North American railroads.

Airbrush equipment manufacturers

Badger Air-Brush Co., 9128 W. Belmont Ave., Franklin Park, IL 60131: Airbrushes, compressors, spray booths, and related equipment.

Binks Mfg. Co., 9201 W. Belmont Ave., Franklin Park, IL 60131: Airbrushes, compressors, spray booths, and related equipment.

North Coast Prototype Models, 28584 E. River Rd., Perrysburg, OH 43551: spray booths and air-abrasive blasters.

Paasche Airbrush Co., 7440 W. Lawrence Ave., Harwood Heights, IL 60656: Airbrushes, compressors, spray booths, and related equipment.

W. R. Brown Co., 901 E. 22nd St., N. Chicago, IL 60064: Airbrushes, compressors, spray booths, and related equipment.

Paint manufacturers:

Accu-paint, SMP Industries, 63 Hudson Rd., P. O. Box 72, Bolton, MA 01740

Accu-Flex (Testor Corp.), 620 Buckbee St., Rockford, IL 61104

Birkholz Meisener (Pro Color), P. O. Box 33, Rochelle, IL 61068

Floquil-Polly S Color Corp., Route 30 N., Amsterdam, NY 12010-9204

Pactra, 1000 Lake Road, Medina, OH 44256

Polly S (see Floquil)

Polly Scale (see Floquil)

Scalecoat, Quality Craft Models, 177 Wheatley Ave., Northumberland, PA 17857

Publications including roster information

Diesel Era magazine, Withers Publishing, 528 Dunkle School Rd., Halifax, PA 17032

Extra 2200 South, Iron Horse Publishers, P. O. Box 8110-820, Blaine, WA 98231-8110

The Official Railway Equipment Register (freight car register), R. E. R. Publishing Corporation, Agent; R. P. DeMarco, Issuing Officer; 424 W. 33rd St., New York, NY 10001

Diesel Locomotive Rosters: U.S., Canada, Mexico, by Charles W. McDonald, Railroad Reference Series No. 9. Kalmbach Publishing Co., P. O. Box 1612, Waukesha, WI 53187.

Index